iPad Air
5th Generation
2022 User Guide

The Complete Instructional Manual for Beginners and

Seniors to Master The iPad Air 5

GW00383844

Howard J. Wall

INTRODUCTION **10**

CHAPTER ONE **12**

FEATURES OF THE IPAD AIR FIFTH GENERATION **12**

CHAPTER TWO **22**

Turn on and set up iPad **22**

Change the settings on your Apple ID 33

Methods for Using iCloud on an iPad 35

Configure your iPad's mail, contacts, and calendar accounts 40

CHAPTER THREE **56**

BASIC **56**

HOW TO COMMUNICATE WITH YOUR IPAD USING BASIC GESTURES. **56**

Learn how to interact with your iPad using advanced gestures. 57

App Library on iPad Air 5 64

How to rearrange home screen pages on the Home Screen 67

How to Change the location where new apps are downloaded. 67

How to open a program from the Dock. 68

How to zoom in an app to make it fill the entire screen. 70

How to close and reopen an app on IPad Air 5. 71

How to drag to copy items on the IPad Air 5 71

How to add a link to a Split View or Slide Over window by dragging it. 72

How to transfer numerous items 74

How to open two objects in Split View on the iPad. . 74

How Change the Split View to a Slide Over 76

How to Return to the full-screen mode................. 77

Move the Slide Over window 80

Turn Slide Over into Split View............................ 81

Open an item in the center of the screen.............. 81

CHAPTER FOUR **83**

windows and workspaces **83**

How to create new windows in an app. 84

How to multitask on the iPad with Picture in Picture.84

Show notification previews on the Lock Screen. 87

How to Use your iPad to conduct a search. 88

How to use Apps to find information 91

CHAPTER FIVE **97**

INFORMATION ON IPAD AIR 5 .... **97**

Create new windows in an app. 98

How to access features from the iPad Lock Screen. 99

How to use your iPad to conduct a search. 102

CHAPTER SIX: **114**

CHANGE OR TURN OFF THE APPLE IPHONE

SOUNDS **114**

Configure the sound settings 114

Silence iPad 114

How to change wallpaper on iPad Air 5. 115

Change the background image. 116

Activate or deactivate Dark Mode. 118

Activate or deactivate Night Shift. 120

How to turn On and Off Focus on Siri. 123

Make a Special Focus. 128

How to modify your notification preferences 130

CHAPTER SEVEN **133**

APP STORE ON IPAD **133**

Purchase and install an app. 134

Connect an iPad to a wireless game controller. 137

Apple Arcade subscription service........................141

Get an App Clip and put it to good use. 143

Modify your App Store preferences. 145

Set content limits and disable in-app purchases. ...146

Text can be highlighted or underlined. 151

Instead of speaking to Siri, type. 161

See what Siri can do on the iPad. 161

Allow Siri to make phone calls. 166

Shortcuts for Siri on iPad 167

Add a recommended shortcut. 167

Make use of a shortcut.......................................168

iPad Siri Suggestions 168

CHAPTER EIGHT **173**

FAMILY SHARING **173**

Make a group for family sharing..........................174

What Can Family Sharing Be Used for? 175

How to create an Apple ID..................................177

How to remove a family member from a group. 178

Create an Apple Cash Family account. 185

Create an Apple Card Family account...................186

CHAPTER NINE **188**

SCREEN TIME **188**

Activate Screen Time..188

Check out your Screen Time summary.................189

Schedule some time away from the computer.......191

CHAPTER TEN **207**

USE IPAD WITH IPHONE, IPOD TOUCH, MAC, AND PC **207**

Create a personal hotspot on your iPad...............207

Use Sidecar 215

Cut, copy, and paste on IPad Air 5 216

CHAPTER ELEVEN... **219**

ACCESSIBILITY **219**

Modify the accessibility options 220

How to turn On Voiceover on IPad Air 5 222

Connect an iPad to a hearing aid. 225

CHAPTER TWELVE **228**

SECURITY AND PRIVACY **228**

How to make a strong password on your IPad Air 5

....228

Learn how to protect yourself from harmful websites

by better understanding the privacy of your browsing

activity in Safari...231

App tracking is under your control......................232

Create a passcode on your iPad. 233

Change the time when the iPad locks automatically.

....234

Disable the passcode 235

Install Face ID on your iPad..............................236

Disable Face ID for the time being.....................237

Install Touch ID on your iPad............................238

CHAPTER 13.. **242**

SAFETY, HANDLING AND SUPPORT.................. **242**

WARNING: 242

Handling: 242

Repairing: 242

Battery: 243

Lasers: 243

Distraction 244

Navigation: 244

Charging: 244

Connector: 245

Long-term heat exposure: 245

USB power: 246

Hearing loss: 247

Exposure: 248

Interference with medical devices: 248

Important iPad handling information..............251

INTRODUCTION

Today, Apple revealed the new iPad Air 5, which includes an Apple-designed M1 CPU that boosts performance significantly. The iPad Air also comes with a new Ultra-Wide front camera with Center Stage for a more natural video conferencing experience, a USB-C port with up to 2x quicker transfer speeds, and blazing-fast 5G on cellular variants – all for the same low price. Users like as content creators, gamers, and students can push the boundaries of creativity, productivity, and self-expression thanks to advanced cameras and compatibility with cutting-edge peripherals. Pre-orders for the new iPad Air begin on Friday, March 11, and the device will be available in shops on Friday, March 18.

"Whether it's a college student taking detailed notes, a content creator working on their latest project, or a gamer playing graphics-intensive games, iPad Air users adore it for its incredible performance and versatility in such a small package," said Greg Joswiak, Apple's senior vice president of Worldwide Marketing. "IPad Air is now more powerful, capable, and simply more enjoyable than ever before, thanks to the innovative M1 chip, Ultra-Wide front camera with Center Stage, and ultra-fast 5G."

CHAPTER ONE

FEATURES OF THE IPAD AIR FIFTH GENERATION

M1 Brings a Massive Leap in Performance to iPad Air

The iPad Air's innovative M1 chip gives even the most demanding apps and workflows a huge speed boost while preserving exceptional power efficiency and all-day battery life. 1 The 8-core CPU gives up to 60% quicker performance than the previous iPad Air, while the 8-core GPU delivers up to 2x faster graphics performance. Advanced machine learning (ML) capabilities are powered by a 16-core Neural Engine, which works in tandem with the CPU and GPU to deliver next-level experiences. M1's performance enables users to do more with iPad Air than ever before, from editing multiple streams of 4K video to playing graphics-intensive games, remodeling a room in 3D, and more realistic augmented reality (AR).

Front-facing camera with a 12MP resolution and an ultra-wide field of view.

The Center Stage Ultra-Wide 12MP front camera automatically pans to keep a good view of users as they move. When more people join the conversation, the camera detects them and zooms out to incorporate them. Center Stage makes connection more interesting than ever before, whether it's reuniting with family or learning online. This spectacular experience is now available on all iPad models, thanks to the inclusion of Center Stage to the iPad Air. 2

The iPad Air's 12MP Wide camera on the rear lets users take clear images and 4K video, as well as scan documents and enjoy amazing augmented reality experiences. The iPad Air is a highly adaptable and ultra-portable mobile studio that offers a complete photo and video capturing, editing, and sharing solution.

Ultra-High-Speed 5G and Advanced Connectivity

Because of the iPad Air's quicker wireless connectivity, customers can do even more with the gadget. The iPad Air can attain peak rates of up to 3.5Gbps over 5G in optimal conditions. 3 The iPad Air gives customers more connectivity options with eSIM and Wi-Fi 6 capabilities, whether they're accessing files, backing up data, interacting with coworkers, or watching a movie with family and friends via SharePlay.

With data speeds of up to 10Gbps, the USB-C connector is now up to two times faster than the previous generation, making it even faster to load huge photographs and videos. The iPad Air's USB-C connector connects it to a growing ecosystem of USB-C peripherals, including cameras, extra storage, and screens with up to 6K resolution.

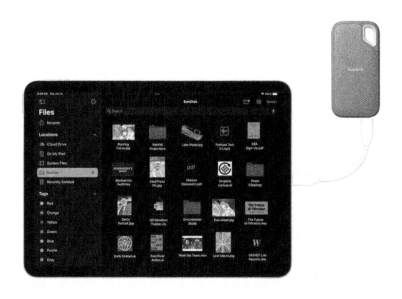

This is an all-screen design with a Liquid Retina Display and Touch ID.

The new iPad Air has been acclaimed for its thin and light design, and it comes in a variety of hues, including space gray, starlight, pink, purple, and a striking new blue. For an immersive visual experience, the iPad Air has a 10.9-inch Liquid Retina display with 3.8 million pixels and innovative technologies as 500 nits of brightness, complete lamination, a P3 broad color gamut, True Tone, and an anti-reflective screen coating. The iPad Air's landscape stereo speakers work in tandem with the Liquid Retina display to produce wide stereo sound for an immersive movie-watching experience. When unlocking the iPad Air, checking in to apps, or using Apple Pay, Touch ID is incorporated into the top button, giving the same simplicity of use and secure authentication that users have come to expect.

Accessories

iPad Air is transformed into a portable digital notebook and sketchbook using Apple Pencil (2nd generation). The wireless charging and pairing capabilities of the Apple Pencil provide pixel-perfect precision and virtually no lag, making writing as effortless and natural as with a pen and paper. Magic Keyboard, with its floating design and integrated trackpad, provides the best typing experience; Smart Keyboard Folio, which provides a comfortable typing experience in a slim design; and Smart Folio covers, which come in coordinating colors — black, white, electric orange, dark cherry, English lavender, and marine blue — that complement the new iPad Air finishes.

iPadOS 15 offers a user interface that is tailored to the iPad's specific features.

- Multitasking has been improved, with features like Split View and Slide Over being easier to find, use, and exploit.
- Notes becomes system-wide with Quick Note, introducing new ways to communicate and organize, whether you're typing or using the Apple Pencil. During a FaceTime chat, SharePlay allows friends and family to share their experiences. Whether users are hosting a viewing party, listening to an album together, or completing a fitness challenge with a friend,

SharePlay keeps everything and everyone completely in sync. iPad's intelligence continues to increase because to powerful machine learning capabilities. Live Text recognizes text in images and prompts users to take action using on-device intelligence. A snapshot of a storefront, for example, may disclose a phone number and the option to call.

- With the release of iPadOS 15.4 and macOS 12.3, users will be able to switch between Mac and iPad using a single mouse and keyboard. Users can also drag and drop information between devices, which is useful for sketching on the iPad with the Apple Pencil and then inserting it into a Keynote deck on the Mac. 5

The iPad Air and the Environment

The enclosure of the iPad Air is fully composed of recycled aluminum, the solder on the main logic board is entirely made of recycled tin, and the enclosure and audio magnets are entirely built of recycled rare earth elements. All iPad models meet Apple's rigorous energy efficiency standards, are free of a variety of dangerous chemicals, and are packaged with wood fiber from from recycled sources or responsibly managed forests.

Apple's global operations are currently carbon neutral, and the company aims to achieve net-zero climate impact across the board by 2030, including manufacturing supply chains and product life cycles. From component production to assembly, transportation, customer usage, and charging, all the way to recycling and material recovery, every Apple gadget sold will be carbon neutral.

Pricing and Availability

- Beginning Friday, March 11, the new iPad Air will be available for pre-order in 29 countries and territories, including the United States, through apple.com/store and the Apple Store app, with availability beginning March 18.
- Wi-Fi models of the iPad Air start at $599 in the United States, while Wi-Fi + Cellular models start at $749. (US). The new iPad Air comes in space gray, starlight, pink, purple, and blue colors, with 64GB and 256GB storage options.
- The new iPad Air comes pre-loaded with iPadOS 15, a sophisticated operating system designed just for iPad. iPadOS 15 is a free software upgrade for iPad Air 2 and subsequent devices.
- Education pricing is accessible at all grade levels for current and newly admitted college students, instructors, staff, and homeschool educators. The new iPad Air has a starting price of $549. (US). The Apple Pencil 2 costs $119 in the United States, the Smart Keyboard Folio costs $159 in the United States, and the Magic Keyboard for college student's costs $279 in the United States (US).

- The Apple Pencil (2nd version) costs $129 and works with the new iPad Air (US).
- The Magic Keyboard for the new iPad Air costs $299 (US) and comes with layouts for more than 30 languages.
- The Smart Keyboard Folio for the new iPad Air is available for $179. (US).
- For $79, you can get the Smart Folio for the new iPad Air in black, white, electric orange, dark cherry, English lavender, and sea blue (US). Once their device is received and validated, Apple will credit their payment method with the value.
- Only at apple.com/store or through the Apple Store app can you personalize your iPad for free with a meaningful combination of emoji, names, initials, and numbers.

Apple provides a wide range of services in-store and online. Apple stores and apple.com/store are the best places to buy Apple products, according to the company. This includes Apple Specialists' customized assistance and advice, as well as easy delivery and pickup options.

CHAPTER TWO

Turn on and set up iPad

Connect your new iPad to the internet and turn it on. Additionally, you can configure iPad by connecting it to your computer. You can transfer your data to your new iPad if you own another iPhone, iPad, iPod touch, or Android device.

Note: If your iPad is being deployed or managed by a business, school, or other organization, seek assistance from an administrator or teacher.

Prepare for installation

To ensure a smooth setup, keep the following items on hand:

wake iPad

To reawaken iPad, perform one of the following actions:

- Hold down the top button.

Top button

- Face ID-enabled iPad unlocking

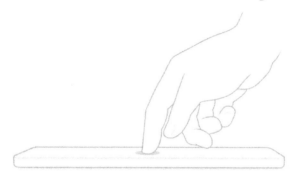

Unlock iPad with Face ID

If you did not configure Face ID during the initial setup of your iPad, see Configure Face ID on iPad.

1. On compatible models, tap the screen and then take a look at your iPad.

To indicate that the iPad has been unlocked, the lock icon animates from closed to open.

2. From the bottom of the screen, swipe up to access the Home Screen.

To reset the iPad's lock, press the top button. If you don't touch the screen for about a minute, the iPad automatically locks. However, if you enable Attention Aware Features in Settings 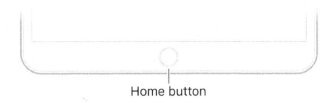 > Face ID & Passcode, iPad will not dim or lock while it detects attention.

iPad Touch ID Unlock

If you did not configure Touch ID during the iPad setup, see Configure Touch ID on iPad.

- On an iPad with a Home button: Press the Home button with the Touch ID-enabled finger.

Home button

- Press the top button to unlock the iPad. If you don't touch the screen for a minute or more, the iPad will automatically lock.

24

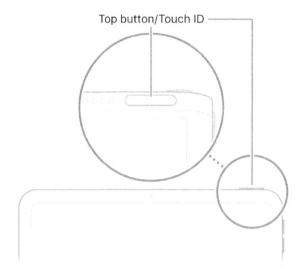

Top button/Touch ID

With a passcode, you may unlock your iPad.

If you didn't set up your iPad with a passcode, check Change or set the passcode.

1. Swipe up from the bottom of the Lock Screen or press the Home button (on an iPad with a Home button) (on other iPad models).
2. Type the passcode into the box.

Press the top button to unlock the iPad. If you don't touch the screen for a minute or more, the iPad will automatically lock.

Install cellular service on your iPad (Wi-Fi + Cellular devices).

You can get a cellular data plan if you have a Wi-Fi + Cellular model. When you're not near a Wi-Fi network, this allows you to stay connected to the internet. Set up a cellular data plan with your carrier.

iPad versions that are supported can connect to 5G networks. See the Apple Support article for further information. With your iPad, use 5G. A SIM card from your carrier is required for the cellular connection. The iPad accepts the following SIM cards:

- eSIM (electronic SIM) (on iPad models that support eSIM; not available in all countries or regions)
- Apple SIM card or embedded Apple SIM
- Your carrier's physical SIM card

With eSIM, you can set up your cellular plan.

You may use your iPad to activate the cellular service on devices that support eSIM. You might be able to use your iPad to travel abroad and sign up for cellular service with a local carrier in the country or region you're visiting. This option is not available in all countries or areas, and it is not supported by all carriers.

1. Go to Cellular Data ⚙ > Settings.
2. Select one of the following options:
- To set up your iPad's initial cellular plan, choose a carrier and then follow the onscreen instructions.
- Tap Add a New Plan to add a new cellular plan to your iPad.
- Tap Other to scan a QR code provided by your carrier. Place iPad in such a way that the QR code provided by your carrier appears in the frame, or manually enter the information. You might be required to input a confirmation code that your carrier has issued.

Install a SIM card.

You can use an Apple SIM card or a carrier-provided SIM.

1. Insert a paper clip or SIM eject tool (not provided) into the SIM tray's small hole, then push the tray toward the iPad to eject it.

SIM tray

Paper clip or
SIM eject tool

The SIM tray's shape and orientation are determined by the iPad model and your country or area.

2. Take the tray off the iPad.
3. Insert the SIM card into the tray. The correct

SIM

   alignment is determined by the angled corner.
4. Replace the tray in the iPad.
5. If you set up a PIN on the SIM before, enter it carefully when required.

   WARNING: Attempting to guess a SIM PIN is dangerous. If you guess incorrectly, your SIM will be permanently locked, and you won't be able to utilize cellular Internet until you receive a new SIM. See the Apple Support article for further information. For your iPhone or iPad, use a SIM PIN.

A wireless data plan is required for cellular data. Contact your carrier to set up service if you're using a third-party SIM.

Organize your cellular data plan.

1. Go to Cellular Data > Settings.
2. Carry out one of the following actions:
- Turn off cellular data and restrict all data to Wi-Fi.
- Tap Cellular Data Options to enable or disable LTE and roaming.
- Enable Personal Hotspot: Select Set Up Personal Hotspot (available from some carriers), then follow the onscreen steps.
- To manage your cellular account, go to Manage [account name] or Carrier Services and select Manage [account name].

iPad should be connected to the internet

Use an available Wi-Fi network to connect your iPad to the internet. Wi-Fi + Cellular models can use a cellular network to connect to the internet.

Join a Wi-Fi network using your iPad.

1. Go to Settings ⚙ > Wi-Fi and switch it on.

2. Select one of the following options:

- A system: If prompted, enter the password.

- Other: Belongs to a secret network. Fill in the hidden network's name, security type, and password.

If a Wi-Fi 📶 network icon displays at the top of the screen, iPad is linked to one. (Open Safari and view a webpage to test this.) When you return to the same spot, the iPad reconnects.

Become a member of a Personal Hotspot

You can use the cellular internet connection of an iPhone or iPad (Wi-Fi + Cellular) that is sharing a Personal Hotspot.

Select the name of the device sharing the Personal Hotspot under Settings ⚙ > Wi-Fi.

If your iPad prompts you for a password, enter the password displayed in Settings ⚙ > Cellular > Personal Hotspot on the device with which you're sharing the Personal Hotspot.

Wi-Fi + Cellular models, Connect iPad to a cellular network

If no Wi-Fi network is available, your iPad automatically connects to your carrier's cellular data network. Check the following if your iPad won't connect:

1. Make sure your SIM card is active and unlocked. Set up cellular service on iPad (Wi-Fi + Cellular variants) for more information.
2. Go to Cellular Data > Settings.
3. Check to see if Cellular Data is turned on.

When you need to connect to the internet, iPad performs the following steps in order until the connection is established:

- Shows a list of accessible Wi-Fi networks in range and connects to the one you choose
- Tries to connect to the most recently used available Wi-Fi network
- Wi-Fi + Cellular models connect to your carrier's cellular data network.

If your iPad supports 5G, it may use your cellular data rather than Wi-Fi. If that's the case, you'll see Using

5G Cellular For Internet beside the name of the Wi-Fi network. Press next to the network name, then tap Use

(i) Wi-Fi for Internet to return to Wi-Fi.

Note: If you don't have access to Wi-Fi, apps and services may send data over your carrier's cellular network, which may incur additional charges. For details on your cellular data plan rates, contact your provider. View or update cellular data settings on iPad (Wi-Fi + Cellular models) to manage cellular data consumption. On the iPad, you can manage your Apple ID settings. Your Apple ID is the username and password you use to log into Apple services like the App Store, iTunes Store, Apple Books, Apple Music, FaceTime, iCloud, I Message, and others.

Use your Apple ID to log in.

Do the following if you didn't sign in during setup:

1. Go to the Settings menu
2. Sign in to your iPad by tapping Sign in.
3. Type your Apple ID and password in the fields provided.

You can create an Apple ID if you don't already have one.

4. Enter the six-digit verification code if your account is protected with two-factor authentication.

Change the settings on your Apple ID

1. Go to [your name] > Settings.
2. Carry out one of the following actions:
- View and adjust your subscriptions
- Update your payment methods or billing address
- Manage Family Sharing
- Update your contact information
- Change your password
- Add or remove Account Recovery Contacts

On the iPad, how do you use iCloud?

iCloud automatically backs up and syncs your photos, videos, documents, backups, and more across all of your devices. You may also share photographs, calendars, notes, folders, and files with family and friends via iCloud. iCloud provides you with an email account as well as 5 GB of free data storage. You can sign up for iCloud+ to get greater storage and features. It's worth noting that some iCloud features have system requirements. The functionality and availability of iCloud vary by country or location.

Make a change to your iCloud preferences.

1. Go to [your name] > Settings > iCloud.

2. Carry out one of the following:

- View the status of your iCloud storage.
- Enable any desired functionality, such as Photos, Mail, Contacts, and Messages.

To learn how to adjust iCloud features on your other devices, visit the iCloud User Guide's Set up iCloud and change settings on all your devices.

Methods for Using iCloud on an iPad

iCloud can automatically back up your iPad. See Make a backup of your iPad. Additionally, you can save and sync the following information in iCloud across your iPad and other Apple devices:

- Photographs and videos; consult Utilize iCloud Photos on your iPad.
- Documents and files; see Configure iCloud Drive on an iPad
- iCloud Mail
- Contacts, Calendars, Notes, and Reminders
- Threaded messages; see Configure Messages on the iPad
- Usernames and passwords, as well as payment methods; see with iPad and iCloud Keychain, you can access your passwords from any device.
- Bookmarks and open tabs in Safari; see Safari on iPad allows you to bookmark favorite websites and utilize tabs.
- Preferences for News, Stocks, and Weather

- Preferences for Home and Health
- Voice memos
- Preferences for Maps

Additionally, you can accomplish the following:

- Upload and share your photographs and movies. See Share iPad photos via iCloud Shared Albums.
- Use iCloud Drive to share folders and documents. See On the iPad, you may share files and folders via iCloud Drive.
- Use Find My to track down a lost device or to share location information with friends and family. See Locate a device and a friend in Find Me on iPad.

Subscribe to iCloud+ for greater storage and access to iCloud Private Relay (beta), Hide My Email, and HomeKit Secure Video functionality.

On iPad, subscribe to iCloud+.

iCloud+ has all of the functionality found in iCloud, plus premium extras such as iCloud Private Relay (beta), Hide My Email, Home Kit Secure Video compatibility, and all of the storage space you need for your images, files, and more. You can purchase iCloud+ separately or as part of Apple One, which includes iCloud+ and more Apple services. Please go to the Apple Support article. Apple subscriptions can be combined with Apple One.

Note: Certain iCloud+ functions have system requirements. iCloud+ and its features are not available in every country or region.

What is included in the iCloud+ subscription?

When you subscribe to iCloud+, the following features become available on iPad:

- Choose from storage capacities of 50 GB, 200 GB, or 2 TB.
- Using Hide My Email, create unique, random email addresses that forward to your personal inbox. See Utilize Hide My Email on the iPad's Safari browser.
- Use Private Relay to browse the web in an even more secure and private manner (beta). See On the iPad, enable iCloud Private Relay.
- Install HomeKit Secure Video on your home security cameras to allow you to access your footage from anywhere while keeping it private

and secure. See Install security cameras in your home using the iPad.

- Personalize iCloud Mail with a custom email domain. The iCloud User Guide contains detailed information on the iCloud+ capabilities and how they work across all of your devices.

Upgrade, your iCloud+ subscription

1. To begin, navigate to Settings ⚙ > [your name] > iCloud.
2. Tap Manage Storage, then tap Change Storage Plan. From there, choose an option and follow the on-screen instructions.

Note: If you cancel your iCloud+ subscription, you will no longer have access to the additional iCloud storage or iCloud+ services.

Distribute iCloud+

Family Sharing enables you to share iCloud+ with up to five other family members. When you share your subscription with family members and they accept, the additional storage and features become instantly available to them. To discontinue sharing iCloud+ with a family group, you can terminate your subscription, leave the family group, or turn off or disable Family Sharing. See On iPad, you can add or remove people from your Family Sharing group. To learn more about bundling your Apple subscriptions with Apple One, visit the Apple Support Article Bundle your Apple subscriptions with Apple One.

Locate the iPad's settings

1. You can search for and adjust iPad settings in the Settings app, such as your passcode, notification tones, and more.

Tap Settings to chang iPad settings (volume screen brightness, an more).

1. From the Home Screen, select Settings (or in the App Library).

2. Swipe down from the top of the screen to expose the search bar; type in a term—for example, "iCloud"—and then tap a setting on the left side of the screen.

Configure your iPad's mail, contacts, and calendar accounts

Along with the apps that come pre-installed on iPad and that you can access through iCloud, iPad works with Microsoft Exchange and a variety of popular web-based mail, contact, and calendar services. You can register for these services.

Establish a mail account

1. To add an account, navigate to Settings 🅰 > Mail > Accounts > Add Account.

2. Take one of the following actions:

- Select an email service, like as iCloud or Microsoft Exchange, and then input your email account credentials.

- Tap Other, then Add Mail Account to create a new account.

Establish a contacts account.

1. 1.To add an account, navigate to Settings > Contacts > Accounts > Add Account > Other.

2. Select Add LDAP Account or Add CardDAV Account (as applicable to your organization), and then enter your server and account information. See Using several contact accounts on an iPad.

Establish a calendar account.

1. To add an account, navigate to Settings 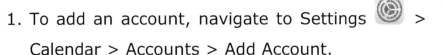 > Calendar > Accounts > Add Account.
2. Select Other and then one of the following:
   - Create a calendar account: Tap Add CalDAV Account, then enter your server and account information; for more information, see Create multiple calendars on iPad.
   - Subscribe to iCal (.ics) calendars: Tap Add Subscribed Calendar, then enter the URL of the.ics file to which you want to subscribe; or import an.ics file from Mail.

When you enable iCloud Keychain on your iPad, your accounts are synced across all of your devices that support iCloud Keychain. In the iCloud User Guide, see Using the iCloud Keychain to keep passwords, accounts, and more up to date using iCloud. Discover the significance of the iPad status icons. The symbols in the top-of-the-screen status bar provide information about iPad.

Note: When a Focus is enabled, its icon displays in the status bar. On the iPad, see Turn a focus on or off. Icon for the current status What does it mean? Wi-Fi The

Status icon   What it means

📶 iPad has a built-in Wi-Fi connection. The stronger the link, the more bars there are.

📶 Wi-Fi network using your iPad. Message from the cell The cellular network is within range of the iPad (Wi-Fi + Cellular variants). "No service" displayed if there is no signal.

✈ Mode of flight The airplane mode is activated. Wireless functions may be deactivated, but no wireless features are available. See Choose iPad settings for travel.

5G 5G Your carrier's 5G network is up and running, and supported models can use it to connect to the internet (not available in all countries or regions). With your iPad, use 5G.

5G UC 5G UC Your carrier's 5G UC network is available, which may include the higher frequency version of 5G offered by your carrier. Over that network, supported models can connect to the internet (not available in all countries or regions). With your iPad, use 5G.

5G+ 5G+ The 5G+ network, which includes your carrier's higher frequency version of 5G, is available. Over that network, supported models can connect to the internet (not available in all countries or regions). See the Apple Support article for further information. With your iPad, use 5G.

5Gᵁᵥᵥ UW 5G The 5G UW network, which may include your carrier's higher frequency version of 5G, is available. Over that network, supported models can connect to the internet (not available in all countries or regions). Use 5G with your iPad, according to Apple Support.

5Gᴱ 5G E Your carrier's 5G E network is live, and supported models can use it to connect to the internet (not available in all countries or regions). View or edit your iPad's cellular data settings (Wi-Fi + Cellular models).

4G The 4G iPad (Wi-Fi + Cellular versions) uses a 4G network to connect to the internet (not available in all countries or regions). See iPad (Wi-Fi + Cellular models): View or modify cellular data settings.

LTE LTE The iPad (Wi-Fi + Cellular versions) uses a 4G LTE network to connect to the internet (not available in all countries or regions).

3G The 3G iPad (Wi-Fi + Cellular versions) uses a 3G network to connect to the internet.

EDGE An EDGE network connects an EDGE iPad (Wi-Fi + Cellular versions) to the internet. See iPad (Wi-Fi + Cellular models): View or modify cellular data settings.

GPRS GPRS The iPad (Wi-Fi + Cellular variants) uses a GPRS network to connect to the internet.

View or edit your iPad's cellular data settings (Wi-Fi + Cellular models). Personal Wi-Fi The iPad is linked to the internet via another device's Personal Hotspot. Turn-by-turn directions are provided by the iPad ⓐ Navigation Indicator. See On the iPad, use Maps to get driving directions.

The iPad's Personal Hotspot Indicator provides a Personal Hotspot. See Your iPad's internet connection (Wi-Fi + Cellular) can be shared.

The iPad is on a phone call, as indicated by the Call Indicator. See On the iPad, you may make and receive phone calls.

The iPad is on a FaceTime call, as indicated by the FaceTime Indicator. See FaceTime calls may be made and received on the iPad.

iPad is recording your screen, as indicated by the Recording Indicator.

See On the iPad, take a screenshot or make a video of the screen.

Indicator of a camera in use Your camera is being used by an app. See Use the camera on your iPad to take pictures.

Indicator of a microphone in use Your microphone is being used by an app.

See Make a recording on your iPad with Voice Memos. Syncing Your iPad is in the process of syncing with your PC.

⛆ See Connect your iPad to your PC. Activity There is some sort of network or other activity going on.

VPN This icon is used by some third-party apps to display app activity. VPN The iPad is connected to a network over a virtual private network (VPN).

🔒 Lock The iPad has been locked. See iPad should be turned on and unlocked.

☎ RTT RTT is activated. See RTT on iPad is easy to set up and use.

🌙 Do Not Interrupt Do Not Disturb is activated. See On the iPad, you can turn on or off the focus.

🔒↻ Locked orientation The orientation of the screen has been locked. See On the iPad, you can change or lock the screen orientation.

➤ Services for finding locations Location Services are being used by an app. See Control the information you share about your location on your iPad.

⏰ Alarm an alarm has been set. See On your iPad, set an alarm.

🎧 Headphones plugged in The iPad is connected to Bluetooth headphones that are turned on and in range. 🔋 See Bluetooth headphones should be set up and listened to. Bluetooth battery displays the battery level of a paired Bluetooth device that is compatible. See On the iPad, set up and use Bluetooth accessories.

🔋 The battery level or charging status is displayed. See Display the percentage of the iPad's battery life.

🔋 The iPad battery is charging, as indicated by the charging icon. See The iPad's battery should be charged.

📺 AirPlay is turned on. See Stream videos and photographs from your iPad to Apple TV or a smart TV wirelessly.

🎤 Voice Commands Siri is ready for your requests now that Voice Control is enabled in Settings > Accessibility. See to interact with the iPad, use Voice Control.

The iPad battery should be charged.

An integrated lithium-ion rechargeable battery powers the iPad. Currently, lithium-ion technology offers the finest performance for your smartphone. Lithium-ion batteries are lighter, charge faster, last longer, and offer a better power density for longer battery life than traditional batteries. Visit the Apple Lithium-ion Batteries website to learn more about how your battery works and how to get the most out of it.

Concerning battery charging

The battery icon in the status bar's top-right corner displays the battery level or charging status. It may take longer to charge the battery when you're syncing or using iPad. If your iPad is running low on battery, it may show an image of a virtually depleted battery, indicating that you must charge it for up to 10 minutes before using it. The display may be blank for up to 2 minutes before the low-battery graphic shows if the iPad is really low on power when you start charging it. See the Apple Support article for further information.

If your iPad won't charge, there are a few things you can do.

The battery should be charged.

Do one of the following to recharge your iPad's battery:

- Using the provided cable and power adapter, connect iPad to a power outlet. See the iPad's included accessories.

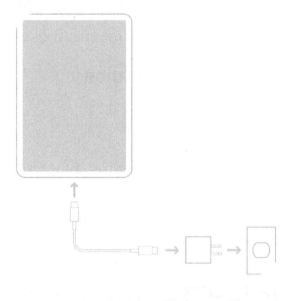

Note: If you plug your iPad into a power outlet, an iCloud backup or wireless computer synchronization will begin. See Make a backup of your iPad and sync it with your PC.

- Use a cable to connect your iPad to your computer. Make sure your computer is turned on; if your iPad is linked to an off computer, the battery may deplete rather than charge. Check the battery symbol ⚡ to see if the iPad is charging.

A Not Charging notice appears in the status bar if your Mac or PC doesn't have enough power to charge iPad. **Note:** Unless your keyboard has a high-power USB connector, don't try to charge your iPad by connecting it to your keyboard.

WARNING: Do not insert the charging cable into the iPad's charging port if you suspect there is liquid inside.

Switch to Low Power Mode.

Low Power Mode can extend the life of a battery charge greatly. When your iPad battery is low or you don't have access to electricity, switch to Low Power Mode.

1. Select Battery from the Settings ⚙ menu.
2. Select Low Power Mode.

Low Power Mode reduces background activities and improves performance for critical operations such as making and receiving phone calls, emails, and messages, surfing the web, and more.

Note: If your iPad automatically goes to Low Power Mode, it will return to standard power mode after charging to 80%. When your iPad is in Low Power Mode, some tasks may take longer.

Display the percentage of the iPad battery life.

In the status bar, you can see how much charge is left in your iPad battery. You can also add a widget to the Home Screen to keep track of your iPad's and connected accessories' battery levels (including Air Pods, Apple Pencil, and more).

In the status bar, you can see the percentage of the iPad's battery life. Go to Settings ⚙ > Battery > Battery Percentage and switch it on.

To your Home Screen, add a Batteries widget.

1. Hold your finger on the Home Screen wallpaper until the apps jiggle.
2. Select Batteries ＋ from the menu at the top of the screen.
3. To see the size options, swipe left and right through the Battery Status widgets.

Information is shown differently depending on the size.

4. When you've found the right size, touch Add Widget, then Done. On the iPad, go to Add Widgets.

Examine your iPad's battery life.

Go to Settings ⚙ > Battery to see how your iPad usage impacts the battery level.

For the last 24 hours and up to 10 days, information on your battery usage and activity is displayed.

- Suggestions and ideas: You may gain knowledge of the conditions or usage patterns that lead iPad to consume energy. You may also come across recommendations for reducing your energy consumption. If a recommendation appears, press it to access the appropriate setting.

- Last Charged: Displays the last time the battery was completely charged as well as the time it was disconnected.

- Last 24 Hours Battery Level Graph: Displays the battery level, charging intervals, and periods when the iPad was in Low Power Mode when the battery was dangerously low.

- Battery Usage Graph (Last 10 Days): Displays the proportion of the battery that has been used each day.
- Activity graph: Displays activity over time, divided by whether or not the screen was on.
- Screen On/Off: Displays total activity for the given time interval, including when the screen was on and off. The average per day is displayed in the Last 10 Days view.
- Battery Usage by App: Displays the percentage of the battery used by each app throughout the time interval specified.
- Activity by App: Displays how much time each app was used during the time interval selected.

Note: Tap a time period in the graph to see battery information for that hour or day. Tap outside the graph to deselect it.

The amount of time a battery lasts and how long it takes to charge it depends on how it's used and how it's Apple or an Apple Authorized Service Provider should service or recycle the iPad battery. Visit the

Battery Service and Recycling page for more information.

Add the instructions to your Home Screen as a shortcut or as a bookmark in Safari for quick access. Tap and then select one of the following options:

- Add to Home Screen (Optional): On the Home Screen, the shortcut displays as a new icon.
- Create a bookmark: When you tap and then tap Bookmarks in Safari, the bookmark appears.
   1. Launch the Books app.
   2. Tap Search, then type "iPad User Guide" in the search box.
   3. Select Get and wait for the book to be downloaded.

See On the iPad, use the Books app to read books.

CHAPTER THREE

BASIC

HOW TO COMMUNICATE WITH YOUR IPAD USING BASIC GESTURES.

Tap, touch and hold, swipe, scroll, and zoom are just a few of the easy gestures that may be used to control iPad and its apps.

Symbol Gesture

Tap. Lightly touch the screen with one finger. Make a connection and hold it. To preview contents and conduct rapid actions in an app, touch and hold the item.

- Touch and hold an app icon on the Home Screen for a few seconds to bring up a quick actions menu.
- Swipe Quickly move one finger across the screen

Scroll Without lifting a finger, move it over the screen. You can, for example, drag a list up or down to see more in Photos. To scroll swiftly, swipe the screen; to stop scrolling, touch the screen. Zoom. Place two fingers near each other on the screen.

Zoom in by spreading them apart, or zoom out by moving them closer together.

Double-tapping a photo or webpage zooms it in, and double-tapping it again zooms it out. Double-tap and hold on Maps, then drag up or down to zoom in or out. If you have a Magic Trackpad or Magic Mouse, see Trackpad gestures for iPad or Mouse actions and gestures for iPad for trackpad and mouse gestures.

Learn how to interact with your iPad using advanced gestures.

Here's a quick guide to the motions you'll use to get to the Home Screen, switch between recent apps, access controls, and more on all iPad models. On an iPad with a Home button, a few motions are performed differently, as seen in the table below.

Gesture Description

Return to your home. To return to the Home Screen at any time, swipe up from the bottom edge of the screen.

See On the iPad, open apps. Controls are easily accessible. To open Control Center, swipe down from the top-right corner; touch and hold a control to see more options. Go to Settings > Control Center to add or remove controls. See Control Center on iPad can be used and customized. Switch to the App Switcher. Swipe up from the bottom border of the screen, pause in the middle, and then lift your finger.

Swipe right to browse the open apps, then press the app you wish to use. See On the iPad, you can switch between apps. Toggle between the open apps. To swiftly navigate between open apps, swipe left or right along the bottom edge of the screen. (Swipe with a little arc on an iPad with a Home button.) See On the iPad, you can switch between apps. Within an app, open the Dock. To expose the Dock, swipe up from the bottom edge of the screen and pause. To open another app quickly, tap it on the Dock. See from the Dock, open an app.

Inquire of Siri. "Hey Siri," all you have to do is say. Alternatively, you can make your request while pressing and holding the top button. (If you have an iPad with a Home button, press and hold it while making your request.) Then let go of the button. See On the iPad, ask Siri a question.

Make use of the Accessibility Shortcut. Click the top button three times. (Triple-click the Home button on an iPad with a Home button.) See On the iPad, use accessibility shortcuts. Take a screenshot of the page. Press and swiftly release the top and volume buttons at the same time. (On an iPad with a Home button, push and swiftly release the top and Home buttons at

the same time.) See On the iPad, take a screenshot or make a video of the screen. Turn off the light. Press and hold the top and volume buttons at the same time until the sliders display, then drag the top slider to power off. (Press and hold the top button on an iPad with a Home button until the sliders show.)

Alternatively, you can navigate to Settings > General > Shut Down. See Switch the iPad on or off (models with the Home button). Restart the computer if necessary. Press and rapidly release the volume button closest to the top button, then press and quickly release the opposite volume button before pressing and holding the top button until you see the Apple logo. The volume buttons on the iPad mini (6th generation) are located in the upper left corner.

See Force the iPad to restart. See Trackpad gestures for iPad or Magic Mouse gestures for iPad if you're using a Magic Trackpad or Magic Mouse. For motions that work with your trackpad or mouse, try the mouse actions and gestures for iPad. iPad loudness can be adjusted.

Adjust the volume of songs and other media, notifications, and sound effects on your iPad with the volume buttons.

(Depending on your model, the volume buttons are on the side or on the top of your device.) You may also use Siri to increase or decrease the volume.

Siri: "Turn up the volume" or "Turn down the volume," for example. Learn how to ask Siri questions. Control Center may be used to turn off audio alerts and notifications.

WARNING: See Vital safety information for iPad for important information on avoiding hearing loss.

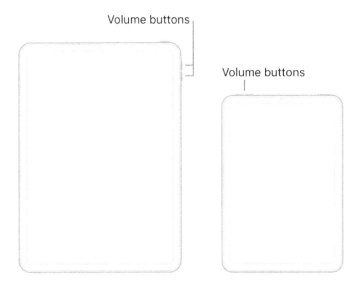

Lock the ringer and turn up the volume on the alarm.

Change with Buttons can be turned off by going to Settings ⚙ > Sounds.

Note: To establish a maximum headset volume restriction, go to Settings > Music > Volume Limit and drag the slider to the desired level.

In Control Center, adjust the volume.

You may control the volume in Control Center whether the iPad is locked or when you're using an app. Open Control Center, then drag 🔊 to the desired location.

Turn off the music.

Hold the Volume Down button down for a few seconds. Silence calls, alarms, and notifications for the time being. Toggle between Focus and Do Not Disturb in Control Center. While listening to headphone audio on an iPad, there are numerous techniques to protect your hearing from excessive noise. See Use the iPad's headphone audio-level features.

iPad apps can be opened.

Apps may be opened fast from your Home Screen pages.

1. Swipe up from the bottom edge of the screen to return to the Home Screen.

2. To browse apps on different Home Screen pages, swipe left or right.

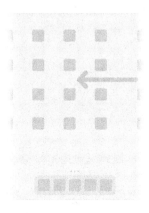

3. Tap an app's icon on the Home Screen to launch it.

4. Swipe up from the bottom edge of the screen to return to the initial Home Screen page.

App Library on iPad Air 5.

Your apps are sorted into categories like Productivity & Finance, Creativity, and Information & Reading in the App Library. You can simply identify and open the apps you use the most because they are towards the top of the screen and at the top level of their categories.

Note: The apps in App Library are intelligently grouped into categories based on how you use them. Apps in App Library can be added to the Home Screen, however they cannot be moved to another category in App Library.

In the App Library, look for and open an app.

1. Open the App Library by going to the Home Screen and swiping left past all of your Home Screen pages.

You may also easily access App Library by touching the Dock's rightmost button at the bottom of the screen.

2. Go to the top of the screen and tap the search field, then type the name of the app you're looking for.

Alternatively, you can scroll through the alphabetical list.

3. Tap an app to open it.

If an App Library category contains a few small app icons, tap them to expand the category and see all of the apps in it.

Home Screen pages can be hidden and seen.

Because all of your apps are stored in App Library, you may not require as many Home Screen pages for apps. Some Home Screen pages can be hidden, bringing App

Library closer to the first Home Screen page. (You can show the hidden pages if you want to see them again.)

1. Hold your finger on the Home Screen until the apps start to bounce.
2. Tap the bottom of the screen's dots. Checkmarks show beneath thumbnail representations of your Home Screen pages.
3. Remove the checkmarks from the pages you want to conceal.

   Tap to add checkmarks to reveal hidden pages.

On an iPad with Face ID, hit Done twice, or tap the Home Screen backdrop twice (on other iPad models).

You can get from the first page of the Home Screen to the App Library (and back) with just one or two swipes now that the other Home Screen pages have been hidden. When Home Screen pages are hidden, new apps from the App Store may be uploaded to the App Library rather than the Home Screen.

How to rearrange home screen pages on the Home Screen

You can rearrange the order of your Home Screen pages if you have more than one. You can, for example, put all of your favorite apps on one Home Screen page and make that your first Home Screen page.

1. Hold your finger on the Home Screen wallpaper until the apps jiggle.
2. Tap the bottom of the screen's dots. Checkmarks show beneath thumbnail representations of your Home Screen pages.
3. Touch and hold each Home Screen page, then drag it to a new location.
4. Press the Done button twice.

How to Change the location where new apps are downloaded.

You can add new apps to the Home Screen and App Library, or just the App Library, when you download them from the App Store.

1. Go to Home Screen & Dock ⊚ > Settings.

2. Select whether new apps should be added to your Home Screen and App Library, or just the App Library.

Turn on Show in App Library to enable app notification badges to appear on apps in the App Library. Add an app to the Home Screen from the App Library.

Unless it's already there, you can add an app from the App Library to the Home Screen.

Tap Add to Home Screen (available only if the app isn't already on the Home Screen) after touching and holding the app.

The app can be found on the Home Screen as well as in the App Library.

On iPad, you can switch between apps.

To rapidly move from one app to another on your iPad, use the Dock, the App Switcher, or a gesture. You can pick up just where you left off when you switch back.

How to open a program from the Dock.

Swipe up from the bottom edge of the screen to display the Dock, then press the app you wish to use. Favorite apps display on the left side of the Dock, while suggested apps (such as those you've recently opened and those open on your iPhone or Mac) appear on the right side. App Library is opened by pressing the rightmost button in the Dock.

Go to App Library

Favorite apps   Suggested apps

1. Use the App Switcher to switch between apps. Do one of the following to see all of your open apps, Split View workspaces, and Slide Over windows in the App Switcher:

- Compatible with all iPad models: Swipe up from the bottom of the screen and then pause in the middle.

- Double-click the Home button on an iPad with a Home button.

2. Swipe right to view the open apps, then press the app or Split View workspace you want to utilize.

By swiping left, you can see the Slide Over windows and press them to swap between them. See Slide Over allows you to switch between apps.

Toggle between the open apps

Do one of the following to switch between open apps:

- With one finger, swipe left or right down the bottom edge of the screen. (On an iPad with a Home button, make a tiny arc with this gesture.)
- Use four or five fingers to swipe left or right.

How to zoom in an app to make it fill the entire screen.

Most iPhone and iPod touch apps will work on the iPad, although they may not take full advantage of the larger screen. To zoom in on the app in this scenario, press.

Return to the original size by ⬈⬋ tapping.

Check the App Store to see if the app ⬊⬉ is available in an iPad version or a universal version that works on iPhone, iPad, and iPod touch.

How to close and reopen an app on IPad Air 5.

If an app isn't responding, you can close it and reopen it to see if the problem is resolved. (Typically, there is no incentive to exit an app; for example, exiting an app does not conserve battery power.)

1. Open the App Switcher, then slide up on the app you want to close.
2. Go to the Home Screen (or the App Library), then press the app to reopen it.

How to drag to copy items on the IPad Air 5

Drag and drop allows you to move text and things within an app and copy items from one app to another with your finger. You can drag an image from Notes into an email, for example. (Drag and drop isn't supported by all third-party programs.)

Make a move with an item

1. Select the item by touching and holding it until it lifts up (if it's text, select it first).
2. Drag it to a different part of the app.

It scrolls automatically if you drag to the bottom or top of a long page.

Copy an item from one app to another.

1. In Split View or Slide Over, open two objects, then touch and hold one of them until it lifts up (if it's text, pick it first).
2. Move it to the other app by dragging it there.

The item appears anywhere you can drop it as you drag. The document scrolls automatically if you drag to the bottom or top of a long document.

Tip: To drag an object to a new note or email, open the note or email first and then drag the item to it.

How to add a link to a Split View or Slide Over window by dragging it.

Touch and hold the link until it rises, then choose one of the options below:

- Replace the link's destination with a Split View or Slide Over window: To open the link, drag it to the window.
- In a Split View or Slide Over window, open the link's destination: Move the link to the left or right side of the screen to open the destination in Split View, or drag the link close to the edge to open in Slide Over, if there is no Split View or Slide Over window visible.

On the Home Screen or in the Dock, copy an item to an app.

1. Select the item by touching and holding it until it lifts up (if it's text, select it first).
2. While holding the item, swipe up from the bottom edge of the screen and stop to display the Dock or click the Home button with another finger (on an iPad with a Home button).
3. To launch the other app, drag the item over it (a ghost image of the item appears under your finger as you ⊕ drag).

You may navigate to where you want to dump an object by dragging it over it in the app (as you drag, appears wherever you can drop the item). You can, for example, drag over the notes list to open the note where you wish to drop the object, or you can use another finger to start a new note where the item can be dropped. Lift your finger before dragging, or drag the item off the screen if you change your mind about moving it.

How to transfer numerous items

1. Touch and hold the first thing you want to choose, then drag it slightly while holding it.
2. Tap additional objects with another finger while still holding the initial item. The number of selected items is indicated by a badge.
3. Combine all of the items by dragging them together. Lift your finger before dragging, or drag the things off the screen if you change your mind about moving them.

How to open two objects in Split View on the iPad.

You can use numerous apps on the iPad at the same time. Split the screen into resizable views to open two independent apps or two windows from the same app. For example, in Split View, open Messages and Maps at the same time. Alternatively, you can use Split View to launch two Messages windows and manage two conversations at once.

In Split View, open a second app.

1. While using an app, tap ⬚ (the three dots at the top of the app), tap, ◼ and then tap to move the current app to the left side of the screen or ◼ the right side of the screen. Your current app slides to the side, revealing your Home Screen and Dock.

2. On your Home Screen or in the Dock, locate the second app you wish to open and tap it.

Split View displays the two apps.

Drag to resize the split.

In Split View, you can swap out an app.

If you have two apps open in Split View, you can swap out one of them for another.

1. Swipe down from the top of the app you want to replace (the three dots at the top of the app).

The app you'd like to replace disappears, and the other app slides to the side, revealing your Home Screen and Dock.

2. Locate and tap the replacement app on your Home Screen or in the Dock.

In Split View, the two programs appear side by side.

How Change the Split View to a Slide Over

When you have two programs or windows open in Split View, you may make one of them a Slide Over window, which slides in front of the other.

To make a Slide Over window, tap at the top of the window you wish to convert, then tap (the rightmost of the three buttons). See in Slide Over, open an app. You can use Split View and Slide Over at the same time on compatible models.

How to Return to the full-screen mode

You can delete one of the apps or windows that are open in Split View and show the other in full screen. Choose one of the following options:

- Drag the center divider to the screen's left or right edge.

- To make an app full screen, tap at the top of the app, then tap.

- To make an app full screen, press and hold the top of the app. Drag it to the middle of the screen, keeping its top edge at the top, until its name and icon appear, then lift your finger.

On the iPad, change an app window to a Slide Over window.

You can switch an app to a Slide Over window (a smaller window that slides in front of another app or window) and start another app behind it while you're using it. For example, you can have Messages open in a Slide Over window while using the Photos app and carry on a conversation while browsing at photos. The iPad remembers which apps you open in Slide Over so you can effortlessly switch between them.

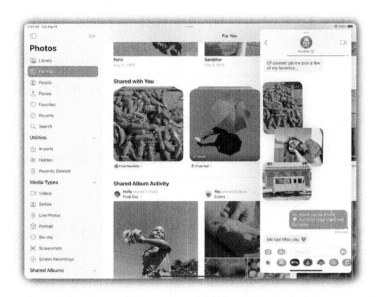

In Slide Over, open an app.

1. Tap at the top of the screen when using an app,

   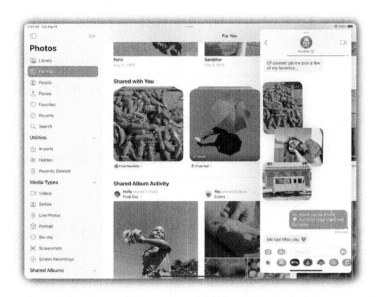 then tap.

Your current app slides to the side, revealing your Home Screen and Dock.

2. Locate and launch the app that will appear behind the Slide Over window.

The second app launches, and the first app appears in front of it in a Slide Over window. When the screen is in Split View and you want to open a third app in Slide Over, pull up from the bottom edge just far enough to reveal the Dock, then drag the third app from the Dock to the Split View divider (on supported models). (See iPad: Open two objects in Split View.)

Slide Over allows you to switch between apps.

Swipe from the top of the Slide Over window to the bottom, or do the following:

1. From the bottom of the Slide Over window, swipe halfway up the screen, pause, and then lift your finger.

All of the Slide Over windows are visible.

2. If the app you wish to see is visible, tap it.

Swipe left and right through the apps if you don't see it.

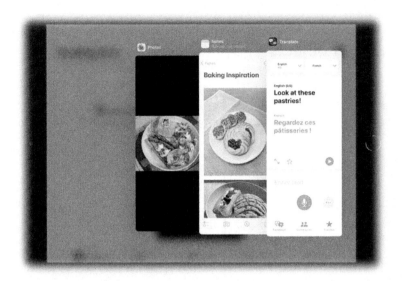

You can also use the App Switcher to switch between apps in Slide Over. See Use the App Switcher.

Move the Slide Over window

Do one of the following:

- *Move the Slide Over window to the other side of the screen:* Drag from ^{...} at the top of the Slide Over window.

- *Temporarily hide the Slide Over window:* Swipe all the way up from the bottom of the Slide Over window, or swipe ^{...}, or drag either side of the window to the left edge of the screen. The Slide Over window disappears and a tab appears to indicate the Slide Over window is still available.

- *Move the Slide Over window back onto the screen:* Drag the tab indicating the Slide Over window from the left edge of the screen.

Turn Slide Over into Split View

Tap ⋯ at the top of the Slide Over window, tap ⊞ , then tap ▣ to have the current app appear on the left side of the screen, or ▣ to place the current app on the right.

On supported models, you can use Slide Over and Split View simultaneously. See Open two items in Split View.

Open an item in the center of the screen

In many iPad apps—including Mail, Messages, Notes, and Files—you can open an item in the center of the app window.

1. Do any of the following:

- Touch and hold a message in a mailbox in Mail.

- Touch and hold a conversation in Messages.

- Touch and hold a note in Notes.

2. Tap Open in New Window.

The item opens in the center of the screen, on top of what you're viewing, without otherwise changing your view.

Tip: You can also pinch open any of the items listed in step 1 above to open them in a new window in the center of the screen. You can change a center window to full screen by tapping , make it a Split View window by tapping , or change it to a Slide Over window by tapping .

CHAPTER FOUR

windows and workspaces

Many iPad apps, like as Mail, Notes, Safari, and Files, allow you to open multiple windows. All open windows in an app, including those in Split View and Slide Over mode, are visible.

In an app, look at the open windows 1.

1. One or more of the following suggestions may be helpful:

   - Swipe up from the bottom edge of the screen to access the Dock.

   - Go to the Home Screen tab.

2. After pressing and holding the program whose windows you want to see, tap Show All Windows.

Note: that if you tap and hold one app for a long time, all of the applications will begin to jitter. Tap Done or touch the Home button to try again (on an iPad with a Home button). Open windows are displayed as thumbnails near the bottom of the screen in some programs. When you tap a thumbnail, the contents of the thumbnail appear in the current full-screen window. To see all of an open app's open windows when using Split View to view apps, press at the top of the open app.

How to create new windows in an app.

When all of an app's open windows appear as thumbnails near the bottom of the screen, you can see $+$ them. Tap it to open a new window in the app. In Split View, tap to show the app's open windows as thumbnails, then $+$ tap.

How to multitask on the iPad with Picture in Picture.

Picture in Picture allows you to watch a video or use FaceTime while using other programs. While watching a video, tap or push the Home button (on an iPad with a Home button). While the video window is shrunk down to a corner of your screen, you may view the Home Screen and access other apps. With the video window open, you can do any of the following:

- Change the size of the video window: pinch open the little video window to expand it. To shrink it again, pinch it closed.

- To enable or disable the controls, tap the video window.

- Drag the video window to a different area on the screen to reposition it.

- To conceal the video window, drag it off the screen's left or right edge.

- Toggle the button to turn off the video window.

- To return to a full-screen video, follow these steps: Tap in the small video box.

You may access features from the iPad Lock Screen.

The Lock Screen appears when you turn on or wake up your iPad, and it displays the current time and date, as well as your most recent notifications. The Lock Screen allows you to receive alerts, enable Camera and Control Center, access information from your favorite apps at a glance, and more.

You may access functions and information from the Lock Screen.

You may use the Lock Screen to quickly access the features and information you need, even if your iPad is locked. To open the camera, swipe left. (See Using the Camera on Your iPad for more details.) To access Control Center, swipe down from the top-right corner. To see past notifications, swipe up from the center. (See View and respond to notifications on the iPad for more information.)

- Start scribbling and taking notes: (On models that are supported) Tap Apple Pencil on the Lock Screen. Anything you produce is saved in Notes.

- For additional information on how to choose what you can access from the iPad Lock

Screen, see Control access to information on the iPad Lock Screen.

Show notification previews on the Lock Screen.

1. Select Notifications > Settings from the drop-down menu.

2. Select Always, then Show Previews from the drop-down menu.

Notification previews include text from Messages, lines from Mail messages, and information about Calendar invitations. See You can view and respond to notifications on the iPad.

Use the iPad to complete quick.

On the Home Screen, Control Center, and in apps, you may see previews, engage quick action choices, and more.

- Press your finger on an image in Photos to receive a preview and a menu of options.

- Touch and hold a message in a mailbox in Mail to see a menu of options and a preview of the message's contents.

- To bring up a quick actions menu, touch and hold an app icon on the Home Screen for a few seconds. If the icons start to jiggle, hit Done or click the Home button (if your iPad has one), then try again.

- Open Control Center and touch and hold an item like Camera or the brightness control to view other options.

- Touch and hold a notification on the Lock Screen for a few seconds to respond.

- Press and hold the Space bar with one finger while typing to turn your keyboard into a touchpad.

How to Use your iPad to conduct a search.

On the iPad, you may look for apps and contacts, as well as content in apps like Mail, Messages, and Photos, as well as text in photos. You may look for and access webpages, photos, and information on artists, performances, TV shows, and movies. You can also perform calculations, such as unit conversions, and double-check stock and currency data. You can search on your iPad from anywhere, including the Lock Screen, and choose which apps appear in search results. Search generates suggestions based on your app usage, and the results update as you type.

Choose which apps will appear in the search results.

1. Go to Siri & Search > Settings ⊚ > Siri & Search > Siri & Search > Siri & Search > Siri

2. To enable or disable Show in Search, scroll down and tap an app.

Searches are carried out on the iPad.

1. Swipe down from the Home Screen or Lock Screen's center.

2. In the search field, type in what you're looking for.

3. Perform one of the following tasks:

   • Hide the keyboard to see the findings on the screen more clearly: Select the Search option.

   • Open a suggested app: It must be tapped.

   • Learn more about a suggestion for a search: Tap it to open it, then tap one of the results to open it.

89

- Start a new search by tapping in the search field.

Search suggestions can be disabled.

In Settings  > Siri & Search, turn off Suggestions while searching.

Turn off Location Services to get recommendations.

1. From the drop-down menu, choose Settings  > Privacy > Location Services.

2. Tap System Services to turn off Location-Based Suggestions.

How to use Apps to find information

Many apps provide a search field or a search button that you can use to find something within the app. In the Maps app, for example, you can look for a specific location.

1. In an app, tap the search area or button (if there is one).

If you don't see a search field or button, swipe down from the top.

2. Begin typing, then press the Search button.

A dictionary should be included.

You can download dictionaries to your iPad and use them to do searches.

1. From the drop-down menu, choose Settings > General > Dictionary.

2. Decide on a dictionary.

Using Airdrop on the iPad, send things to nearby devices.

Airdrop allows you to send images, videos, URLs, locations, and more to other nearby devices and Mac PCs (iOS 7, iPadOS 13, OS X 10.10, or later required). To transfer data, Airdrop requires both Wi-Fi and Bluetooth to be turned on. To use Airdrop, you must be logged in with your Apple ID. All transfers are encrypted to protect security.

You can utilize Airdrop to send something.

1. To open the item, tap Share, AirDrop, or another button that displays the app's sharing options.

2. In the row of sharing options, tap the profile image of a nearby Airdrop user.

If they don't appear as a nearby AirDrop user, ask them to open Control Center on their iPhone, iPad, or iPod touch and allow AirDrop to receive objects. To send to a Mac user, utilize AirDrop to request that they enable themselves to be discovered in the Finder. To send something other than an AirDrop item, select a method from the list of sharing choices, such as Messages or Mail (options vary by app). Siri may suggest methods to share with people you know by presenting their profile photos and icons that represent sharing choices. You can also use AirDrop to send secure app and website credentials to someone with an iPhone, iPad, iPod touch, or Mac. See Passwords can be safely shared on the iPad via AirDrop.

Allow others to send things to your iPad via AirDrop.

1. Tap and hold the top-left group of controls in Control Center.

2. Tap Contacts Only or Everyone to select who you want to receive messages from.

As requests come in, you have the choice of accepting or denying them.

Note: that the Contacts Only option is only available on devices running iOS 10, iPadOS, or macOS 10.12 or later. To receive objects using AirDrop if your device's AirDrop is set to Contacts Only on a previous software version, go to Control Center and select the Everyone option. You can pick the Everyone option when using AirDrop and turn it off when not in use. Take a screenshot or record a video of the screen on the iPad. You can take a snapshot of the screen exactly as it appears, or a video of actions on the screen, to share with colleagues or use in papers.

Make a photograph of it.

1. Complete one of the tasks below:

   - Press and release the top button (on the top-right side of the iPad) and either volume button at the same time on an iPad with a Home button; on other iPad models, press and release the top button (on the top-right side of the iPad) and either volume button at the same time.

2. Select Done, then select the screenshot from the lower-left corner.

3. Choose from the Save to Photos, Save to Files, or Delete Screenshot options.

If you pick Save to Photos, it will appear in the Screenshots album in the Photos app, or in the All Photos album if you're using iCloud Photos.

From a full-page screenshot, create a PDF.

Take a full-page, scrolling snapshot of a webpage, document, or email that is longer than the length of your iPad screen to save a PDF.

1. Complete one of the tasks below:

- Press and release the top button and the Home button at the same time on an iPad with a Home button; on other iPad models, press and release the top button and either volume button at the same time.

2. Select Full Page, then select the screenshot in the bottom-left corner.

3. Perform one of the following tasks:

   - To save the screenshot, press Done, then Save PDF to Files, choose a place, and then tap Save.

   - Distribute the screenshot to as many people as possible: Select a sharing option (such as Airdrop, Messages, or Mail), then fill out any other required fields before sending the PDF.

Take a screenshot of the screen.

You can capture voice and produce a screen recording on your iPad.

1. Select Screen Recording from the Settings > Control Center menu.

2. Tap ⊙ Control Center to start the countdown, then wait three seconds.

3. To stop recording, open Control Center, tap ⊙ the red status bar at the top of the screen, then tap Stop. From the Photos ✿ menu, choose your screen recording.

CHAPTER FIVE

INFORMATION ON IPAD AIR 5

Many iPad apps, like as Mail, Notes, Safari, and Files, allow you to open multiple windows. All open windows in an app, including those in Split View and Slide Over mode, are visible.

1. In an app, look at the open windows 1.

One or more of the following suggestions may be helpful:

- Swipe up from the bottom edge of the screen to access the Dock.
- Go to the Home Screen tab.

2. After pressing and holding the program whose windows you want to see, tap Show All Windows.

Note that if you tap and hold one app for a long time, all of the applications will begin to jitter. Tap Done or touch the Home button to try again (on an iPad with a Home button). Open windows are displayed as thumbnails near the bottom of the screen in some programs. When you tap a thumbnail, the contents of the thumbnail appear in the current full-screen window. To see all of an open app's open windows when using Split View to view apps, press at the top of the open app.

Create new windows in an app.

When all of an app's open windows appear as thumbnails near the bottom of the screen, you can see them. Tap it to open a new window in the app. In Split View, tap to show the app's open windows as thumbnails, then tap. You can multitask on the iPad with Picture in Picture. Picture in Picture allows you to watch a video or use FaceTime while using other programs. While watching a video, tap or push the Home button (on an iPad with a Home button). While the video window is shrunk down to a corner of your screen, you may view the Home Screen and access other apps. With the video window open, you can do any of the following

• Change the size of the video window: pinch open the little video window to expand it. To shrink it again, pinch it closed.

• To enable or disable the controls, tap the video window.

• Drag the video window to a different area on the screen to reposition it.

    • To conceal the video window, drag it off the screen's left or right edge.

    • Toggle the button to turn off the video window.

    • To return to a full-screen video, follow these steps: Tap in the small video box.

How to access features from the iPad Lock Screen.

The Lock Screen appears when you turn on or wake up your iPad, and it displays the current time and date, as well as your most recent notifications. The Lock Screen allows you to receive alerts, enable Camera and Control Center, access information from your favorite apps at a glance, and more.

Tap to turn on airplane mode.

You may access functions and information from the Lock Screen. You may use the Lock Screen to quickly access the features and information you need, even if your iPad is locked. To open the camera, swipe left. To access Control Center, swipe down from the top-right corner. (See Control Center for the iPad: Use and Customize for more details.)

To see past notifications, swipe up from the center. (See View and respond to notifications on the iPad for more information.)

- Start scribbling and taking notes: (On models that are supported) Tap Apple Pencil on the

Lock Screen. Anything you produce is saved in Notes.

For additional information on how to choose what you can access from the iPad Lock Screen, see Control access to information on the iPad Lock Screen.

Show notification previews on the Lock Screen.

1. Select Notifications > Settings from the drop-down menu.
2. Select Always, then Show Previews from the drop-down menu.

Notification previews include text from Messages, lines from Mail messages, and information about Calendar invitations. See You can view and respond to notifications on the iPad. On the Home Screen, Control Center, and in apps, you may see previews, engage quick action choices, and more.

- Press your finger on an image in Photos to receive a preview and a menu of options.
- Touch and hold a message in a mailbox in Mail to see a menu of options and a preview of the message's contents.

- To bring up a quick actions menu, touch and hold an app icon on the Home Screen for a few seconds. If the icons start to jiggle, hit Done or click the Home button (if your iPad has one), then try again.
- Open Control Center and touch and hold an item like Camera or the brightness control to view other options.
- Touch and hold a notification on the Lock Screen for a few seconds to respond.
- Press and hold the Space bar with one finger while typing to turn your keyboard into a touchpad.

How to use your iPad to conduct a search.

On the iPad, you may look for apps and contacts, as well as content in apps like Mail, Messages, and Photos, as well as text in photos. You may look for and access webpages, photos, and information on artists, performances, TV shows, and movies. You can also perform calculations, such as unit conversions, and double-check stock and currency data. You can search on your iPad from anywhere, including the Lock Screen, and choose which apps appear in search results. Search generates suggestions based on your app usage, and the results update as you type.

Choose which apps will appear in the search results.

1. Go to Siri & Search > Settings > Siri & Search > Siri & Search > Siri & Search > Siri

2. To enable or disable Show in Search, scroll down and tap an app.

Searches are carried out on the iPad.

1. Swipe down from the Home Screen or Lock Screen's center.

2. In the search field, type in what you're looking for.

3. Perform one of the following tasks:

   - Hide the keyboard to see the findings on the screen more clearly: Select the Search option.

   - Open a suggested app: It must be tapped.

   - Learn more about a suggestion for a search: Tap it to open it, then tap one of the results to open it.

- Start a new search by tapping in the search field.

Search suggestions can be disabled.

In Settings > Siri & Search, turn off Suggestions while searching.

Turn off Location Services to get recommendations.

1. From the drop-down menu, choose Settings > Privacy > Location Services.
2. Tap System Services to turn off Location-Based Suggestions.

Apps for finding information

Many apps provide a search field or a search button that you can use to find something within the app. In the Maps app, for example, you can look for a specific location.

3. In an app, tap the search area or button (if there is one). If you don't see a search field or button, swipe down from the top.

   Begin typing, then press the Search button.
1. From the drop-down menu, choose Settings > General > Dictionary.
2. Decide on a dictionary.

Using Airdrop on the iPad, send things to nearby devices. Airdrop allows you to send images, videos, URLs, locations, and more to other nearby devices and Mac PCs (iOS 7, iPadOS 13, OS X 10.10, or later required). To transfer data, Airdrop requires both Wi-Fi and Bluetooth to be turned on. To use Airdrop, you must be logged in with your Apple ID. All transfers are encrypted to protect security.

You can utilize Airdrop to send something.

1. To open the item, tap Share, Airdrop, or another button that displays the app's sharing options.
2. In the row of sharing options, tap the profile image of a nearby Airdrop user.

If they don't appear as a nearby Airdrop user, ask them to open Control Center on their iPhone, iPad, or iPod touch and allow Airdrop to receive objects. To send to a Mac user, utilize Airdrop to request that they enable themselves to be discovered in the Finder.

To send something other than an Airdrop item, select a method from the list of sharing choices, such as Messages or Mail (options vary by app). Siri may suggest methods to share with people you know by presenting their profile photos and icons that represent sharing choices. You can also use Airdrop to send secure app and website credentials to someone with an iPhone, iPad, iPod touch, or Mac. See Passwords can be safely shared on the iPad via Airdrop.

Allow others to send things to your iPad via Airdrop.

1. Tap and hold the top-left group of controls in Control Center.
2. Tap Contacts Only or Everyone to select who you want to receive messages from.

As requests come in, you have the choice of accepting or denying them.

Note that the Contacts Only option is only available on devices running iOS 10, iPadOS, or macOS 10.12 or later. To receive objects using Airdrop if your device's Airdrop is set to Contacts Only on a previous software version, go to Control Center and select the Everyone option. You can pick the Everyone option when using Airdrop and turn it off when not in use.

Take a screenshot or record a video of the screen on the iPad. You can take a snapshot of the screen exactly as it appears, or a video of actions on the screen, to share with colleagues or use in papers.

Make a photograph of it.

1. Complete one of the tasks below:
   - Press and release the top button (on the top-right side of the iPad) and either volume button at the same time on an iPad with a Home button; on other iPad models, press and release the top button (on the top-right side of the iPad) and either volume button at the same time.
2. Select Done, then select the screenshot from the lower-left corner.
3. Choose from the Save to Photos, Save to Files, or Delete Screenshot options.

If you pick Save to Photos, it will appear in the Screenshots album in the Photos app, or in the All Photos album if you're using iCloud Photos.

From a full-page screenshot, create a PDF.

Take a full-page, scrolling snapshot of a webpage, document, or email that is longer than the length of your iPad screen to save a PDF.

1. Complete one of the tasks below:
   - Press and release the top button and the Home button at the same time on an iPad with a Home button; on other iPad models, press and release the top button and either volume button at the same time.
2. Select Full Page, then select the screenshot in the bottom-left corner.
3. Perform one of the following tasks:
   - To save the screenshot, press Done, then Save PDF to Files, choose a place, and then tap Save.
   - Distribute the screenshot to as many people as possible: Select a sharing option (such as AirDrop, Messages, or Mail), then fill out any other required fields before sending the PDF.

Take a screenshot of the screen.

You can capture voice and produce a screen recording on your iPad.

1. Select Screen Recording from the Settings > Control Center menu.
2. Tap Control Center to start the countdown, then wait three seconds.

3. To stop recording, open Control Center, tap the red status bar at the top of the screen, then tap Stop.

4. From the Photos menu, choose your screen recording.2. Carry out one of the following actions:

- Type on the onscreen or wireless keyboard after tapping in the note. See Use your iPad to take notes.

- Enter text using the Apple Pencil and Scribble. See Scribble is an iPad app that allows you to enter text.

Typed text can be added to and edited in other supported apps.

1. Tap in the Markup toolbar, then Text.

Note: If the Markup toolbar isn't visible in a compatible app, tap or Markup. Tap the minimized version of the toolbar if it is minimized.

2. Tap twice on the text box.

3. Enter text using the keyboard.

After you've added typed text, tap it to select it, then perform one of the following:

- Change the font, size, or layout: Select an option from the toolbar.
- Change the text by deleting, editing, or duplicating it: Select a choice after tapping the text.
- Drag the text to reposition it.

When you're done, touch or Done to hide the Markup toolbar.

In other supported apps, you can add and alter a shape.

1. Tap in the Markup toolbar, then select a shape.

   Note: If the Markup toolbar isn't visible, tap or Markup. Tap the minimized version of the toolbar if it is minimized.

2. To change the shape, choose one of the following options:
   - Drag the shape to move it.
   - Resize the form by dragging any blue dot around the outline of the shape.
   - To change the color of the outline, select a color from the color picker.

- Change the line thickness or fill the shape with color by tapping, then selecting an option and a color.
- Drag a green dot to change the shape of an arrow or a speech bubble.
- To delete or duplicate a shape, simply tap it and select an option.

When you're done, touch or Done to hide the Markup toolbar. Add your signature to other apps that support it.

1. Tap in the Markup toolbar, then select Signature.
2. Note: If the Markup toolbar isn't visible, tap or Markup. Tap the minimized version of the toolbar if it is minimized.

Select one of the following options:

- Create a new signature by tapping Add or Remove Signature, then signing your name with the Apple Pencil or your finger.

Tap Done to use the signature, or Clear to create a new one.

- To add an existing signature, select the one you want and tap it.

Scroll down the list to view all of your signatures.

3. Drag your signature to the desired location.

When you're done, touch or Done to hide the Markup toolbar. You can write text in any field in iPad apps that support Markup and have it instantly transformed to typed text. On the iPad, see Enter text using Scribble.

In Markup on iPad, you may magnify or zoom in.

When using Markup in supported apps, you can zoom in to sketch the finer details. When you simply need to view the finer details, use the magnifier. Pinch open while using Markup in a compatible app to draw, modify shapes, and more up close. Drag two fingers to pan when you're zoomed in. Pinch closed to zoom back out.

Magnify

In a compatible app (other than Notes), tap and then Magnifier in the Markup toolbar.

Note: If the Markup toolbar isn't visible, tap or Markup. Tap the minimized version of the toolbar if it is minimized. Change the properties of the magnifier by doing one of the following:

- Increase or decrease the magnification level: On the magnifier, drag the green dot.
- To change the magnifier's size, drag the blue dot on the magnifier.
- Drag the magnifier to move it.
- To change the magnifier's outline thickness, tap and then select an option.
- Change the color of the magnifier's outline by using the color picker.
- To delete or duplicate the magnifier, first tap its outline, then select Delete or Duplicate from the menu.

When you're done, touch or Done to hide the Markup toolbar.

CHAPTER SIX:

CHANGE OR TURN OFF THE APPLE IPHONE SOUNDS

Change or disable the sounds that iPad makes when you receive a call, text message, email, reminder, or other sort of notification in Settings. Turn on Do Not Disturb to temporarily quiet incoming calls, alarms, and sound effects.

Configure the sound settings

Set the ringer and alert volumes, as well as the alert tones and ringtones.

1. Go to Sounds > Settings.
2. Adjust the volume of the ringer and alerts by dragging the slider.
3. Select sounds for the ringtone and alert tones by tapping Ringtone and other choices.

Silence iPad

Open Control Center, hit Focus, then tap Do Not Disturb to temporarily stop incoming calls, alarms, and sound effects. If you're not getting incoming calls and notifications when you should, click Control Center and make sure Do Not Disturb is turned on 🌙. Toggle off Do Not Disturb if it is highlighted. (Do Not Disturb is also displayed in the status bar when Do Not Disturb is enabled.) 🌙

How to change wallpaper on iPad Air 5.

Choose a wallpaper for the iPad's Lock Screen or Home Screen by selecting an image or photo. There are both dynamic and stationary photos to pick from.

Change the background image.

1. Select a new wallpaper by going to Settings > Wallpaper > Choose a New Wallpaper.

2. Carry out one of the following actions:

- At the top of the screen, select a preset image from a group (Dynamic, Stills, and so on).

- When Dark Mode is enabled, the wallpaper tagged with changes appearance.

- Choose a photo from your own collection (tap an album, then tap the photo).

Pinch open your picked image to zoom in on it, then drag it around to reposition it. To zoom out, pinch closed.

- Tap to enable Perspective Zoom (available with select wallpaper options), which causes your wallpaper to appear to "move" as your viewing angle changes.

If Reduce Motion (in Accessibility options) is enabled, the Perspective Zoom option will not appear. For more information, see Customize iPad for Motion Sensitivities.

Tap Set, then select one of the options:

- Turn on the lock screen
- Configure the Home Screen
- Configure both

Go to Settings > Wallpaper, tap the image on the Lock Screen or Home Screen, then tap Perspective Zoom to enable Perspective Zoom for wallpaper you've already set. On the iPad, adjust the screen brightness and color. You may dim or brighten the screen on your iPad (dimming the screen extends battery life). Dark Mode, True Tone, and Night Shift can also be used to manually or automatically modify the screen color and brightness.

Manually adjust the screen brightness.

Do one of the following to make your iPad's screen darker or brighter:

- First, open Control Center, and then drag
- Select Display & Brightness from the Settings menu, then drag the slider.

Automatically adjust the screen brightness

Using the built-in ambient light sensor, iPad adjusts the screen brightness to match the current lighting conditions.

1. Select Accessibility from the drop-down menu under Settings.
2. Turn on Auto-Brightness under Display & Text Size.

Activate or deactivate Dark Mode.

Dark Mode applies a dark color palette to the whole iPad experience, making it ideal for low-light situations. You may use your iPad in Dark Mode while reading in bed, for example, without disturbing the person next to you.

Try one or more of the following:

- To toggle Dark Mode on or off, open Control Center, touch and hold, then tap.
- Go to Settings > Display & Brightness, then pick Dark or Light to enable or disable Dark Mode.

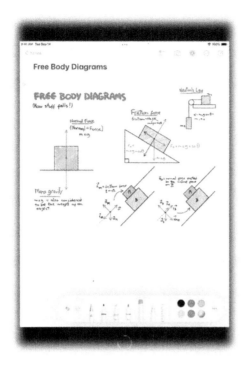

Dark Mode can be set to switch on and off automatically. In Settings, you can have Dark Mode switch on automatically at night (or on a specified schedule).

1. Select Display & Brightness from the Settings menu.
2. Select Automatic, then Options.
3. Select either Sunset to Sunrise or Custom Schedule from the drop-down menu.

If you select Custom Schedule, use the choices to program when Dark Mode will switch on and off.

If you choose Sunset to Sunrise, iPad determines when it's evening for you based on your clock and locality.

Activate or deactivate Night Shift.

You may manually activate Night Shift, which is useful if you're in a darkened room during the day.

Touch and hold to open Control Center, then tap to close it.

Night Shift can be set to turn on and off automatically.

Schedule Night Shift to make viewing the screen easier on your eyes by shifting the colors in your display to the warmer end of the spectrum at night.

1. Select Display & Brightness > Night Shift from the Settings menu.
2. Select Scheduled from the drop-down menu.
3. Drag the slider below Color Temperature toward the warmer or cooler end of the spectrum to modify the color balance for Night Shift.
4. Select Sunset to Sunrise or Custom Schedule from the form menu.

If you select Custom Schedule, use the choices to program when Night Shift will switch on and off. If you choose Sunset to Sunrise, iPad determines when it's evening for you based on your clock and locality.

Note that if you turned off Location Services in Settings > Privacy or Setting Time Zone in Settings > Privacy > Location Services > System Services, the Sunset to Sunrise option will be unavailable.

True Tone can be turned on or off.

True Tone intelligently adjusts the color and intensity of your display to match the light in your environment on compatible models.

- To turn True Tone on or off, open Control Center, touch and hold, then tap.
- Select Display & Brightness from the Settings menu, then toggle True Tone on or off.

Display Zoom enlarges the iPad screen.

Display Zoom on the iPad Pro 12.9-inch magnifies the screen display.

1. Select Display & Brightness from the Settings menu.
2. Select View (below Display Zoom).
3. Tap Set after selecting Zoomed.

On the iPad, you can turn on or off the focus.

You may turn on a Focus manually or set it to turn on automatically in Control Center.

In Control Center, turn on a focus.

1. Open Control Center, select Focus, and then select the Focus you want to activate (for example, Do Not Disturb).

If another Focus is currently active when you tap the new one, it will be turned off.

2. To choose an end point for the Focus, tap the icon next to it, select an option (such as "For 1 hour" or "Until I leave this location"), and then tap again. When you turn on a Focus, the icon for that Focus (for example, Do Not Disturb) displays in the status bar and on the Lock Screen, and your status is automatically displayed in the Messages app. Your friends will be able to see that you have turned off notifications, but they will still be able to contact you if there is an emergency. Note: You can also enable or disable a Focus by navigating to Settings > Focus, touching the Focus, and then

enabling it. Siri can be used to turn on or off a Focus.

How to turn On and Off Focus on Siri.

Siri: "Turn on the Work Focus," or "Turn off the Work Focus," for example. Learn how to ask Siri questions.

Set a Focus to turn on automatically on a regular basis.

You may set a Focus to turn on at specific moments, such as when you arrive at a given area or when you open a specific app.

1. Go to Settings > Focus and select the Focus you'd like to schedule.
2. Tap Add Schedule or Automation, then provide the hours, a place, or an app to which this Focus should be activated.
3. Tap Smart Activation, switch on Smart Activation, then tap at the top to have this Focus turn on automatically based on indications like your location, app usage, and more.

Note: When you set up a Sleep Focus on your iPhone, it will follow the sleep schedule you set up in the Health App. Open the Health app on your iPhone, tap Browse, then Sleep to add or update a sleep schedule.

Disable a Focus

When you're done with a Focus, swiftly turn it off to resume receiving notifications. Even if you switch off a Focus, it remains in Control Center and can be utilized again.

1. Complete one of the following tasks:
- Open Control Center, then tap Focus after touching and holding the Focus icon on the Lock Screen.
2. Toggle off the Focus that is currently active.

Remove a focal point

You can erase a Focus you've created if you don't need it anymore.

1. Select Settings > Focus from the drop-down menu.
2. Tap the Focus, then tap Delete Focus at the bottom of the screen.

If you erase a Focus, you'll have to re-enable it by heading to Settings > Focus and touching.

Set up a Focus on iPad A focus is a function on the iPad that helps you focus on a task by reducing distractions.

Focus can temporarily quiet all notifications—or allow only particular notifications (for example, ones that match your task)—and let other people and applications know you're busy when you need to focus or step away from your iPad.

You can select from a menu of Focus options or construct your own.

Note: To silence all notifications instantly, open Control Center, hit Focus, and then toggle Do Not Disturb on. Do Not Disturb, Do Not Disturb, Do Not Disturb, Do Not Disturb, Do Not Disturb Driving is now a component of Focus.

Create a Focus

You can tweak a predefined Focus option—for example, Do Not Disturb, Personal, Sleep, or Work— or establish a Custom Focus when you wish to focus on a certain activity. Set up Work Focus and only accept alerts from your peers and the apps you need for work. Similarly, you can create a Home Screen page with only apps linked to your Focus and make it the only page available during your Focus.

1. Select Settings ⚙ > Focus from the drop-down menu.

2. Select a Focus, such as Do Not Disturb, Personal, Sleep, or Work, and then follow the on-screen instructions.

3. After you've created your Focus, go to Settings > Focus and edit any of the following (which are initially set when you establish your Focus):

- Select the persons from whom you'd like to receive notifications (if any) during this Focus: Select contacts by tapping People (or Add Person), then touch Done.

- Decide whether or not you want to be contacted during this Focus: Select Everyone, No One, Favorites, or All Contacts from the Calls from menu. Allow Repeated Calls is turned on to allow two or more calls from the same individual within three minutes. Then tap on the top left corner.

Note: Calls from your emergency contacts will always come through, regardless of your Focus settings. See When notifications are turned off, allow calls from emergency contacts.

- Select which apps (if any) you wish to get notifications from during this Focus: Select apps by tapping Apps or Add App, then touch Done.
- During this Focus: Choose if you want to allow all applications to send you time-sensitive notifications right away. Toggle on Time Sensitive, then tap in the upper left corner.
- Select whether you want apps to be able to see that you've turned off notifications: Turn Share Focus Status on or off by tapping Focus Status. When you switch it on, people who message you will see that your alerts are turned off, but they won't know which Focus you're using.
- During this Focus, select the Home Screen sites you want to visit: Select the Home Screen pages you wish to utilize during this Focus by tapping Home Screen, turning on Custom Pages, then tapping Done.

Tip: You can transfer all of the apps for this Focus to a single Home Screen page and then pick that page.

- Display silent alerts on the Lock Screen or dim the Lock Screen: Turn on Show On Lock Screen by tapping Lock Screen. You can also darken the

Lock Screen during this Focus by turning on Dim Lock Screen.

You may utilize a Focus once you've set it up by turning it on in Control Center or scheduling it to turn on automatically. When you set up a Sleep Focus, it will follow your iPhone's Sleep routine. Open the Health app on your iPhone, tap Browse, then Sleep to add or update your sleep routine.

Make a Special Focus

You can construct a Custom Focus if you wish to focus on an activity that isn't covered by any of the available Focus options.

1. Select Settings > Focus from the drop-down menu.
2. Tap Custom in the top right corner.
3. Give your Focus a name, then press Return.
4. Tap Next after selecting a color and a symbol to represent your Focus.
5. Make any of the options given in Step 3 of the Set up a Focus section above your own.

Keep all of your Apple devices' Focus settings up to date. All of your Apple devices that are logged in with the same Apple ID can use the same Focus settings.

1. Select Settings > Focus from the drop-down menu.
2. Select Share Across Devices and turn it on.

When notifications are turned off, allow calls from emergency contacts.

Even if your iPad or notifications are turned off, you can allow noises from emergency contacts to get through.

1. Make a list of all of your contacts.
2. Tap Edit after selecting a contact.
3. Turn on Emergency Bypass by tapping Ringtone or Text Tone.

On the iPad, change the notification settings.

Choose which apps are allowed to send notifications, adjust the alert sound, set up location-based alerts, authorize government alerts, and more in Settings.

How to modify your notification preferences

Each app's notification settings can be adjusted in most cases. You may turn on or off app notifications, have them play a sound, customize how and where app alerts appear when your device is opened, and more.

1. Go to Notifications > Settings.
2. To plan a notification summary, go to Notifications > Scheduled Summary > Scheduled Summary > Scheduled Summary > Scheduled Summary > Scheduled Summary > Scheduled Summary > Scheduled Summary > Scheduled Summary > Schedule

Select the applications for which you want notifications in your summary, set a time for your summary to be sent, and then touch in the top left. (For more information, see the schedule a notice summary.)

3. Tap Show Previews, select an option—Always, When Unlocked, or Never—then tap at the upper left to specify when most notification previews appear.

Text (from Messages and Mail) and invitation details can be included in previews (from Calendar). This parameter can be overridden for specific apps.

> 4. Turn Allow Notifications on or off by tapping an app below Notification Style.

If you enable Allow Notifications, you can specify when you want the notifications to be delivered—immediately or in the planned notifications summary—as well as whether you want Time Sensitive Notifications enabled or disabled.

You may also change the notification banner style and turn on or off noises and badges for various apps.

> 5. Choose how you want the notifications to be organized by tapping Notification Grouping.

- Automatic: The app's notifications are classified according to the app's organizational criteria, such as topic or thread.
- By App: All of the app's alerts are grouped together.
- Off: Disable grouping.

Go to Settings > Notifications > Siri Suggestions, then turn off any app to turn off notifications for specific apps. When you use Focus on your iPad, it pauses the transmission of notifications to avoid interruptions.

CHAPTER SEVEN

APP STORE ON IPAD

Tap any of the following to find apps, games, and in-app events:

- Today: Look through today's featured content, apps, and in-app events.
- Games: Choose from dozens of categories to choose your next game, including action, adventure, racing, puzzles, and more.
- Apps: See what's new, check out the top charts, or browse by category.
- Arcade: Play Apple Arcade's curated library of premium games without commercials or in-app purchases (membership required).
- Search: Type in what you're looking for and then press the Search key on your keyboard.

"Search the App Store for cooking apps," for example, or "Get the Minecraft app," according to Siri. Learn how to ask Siri questions.

Find out more about an app.

To see the following information and more, tap an app:

- Screenshots or sneak peeks
- Game Center and Family Sharing support
- Compatibility with other Apple devices
- In-app events
- Ratings and reviews
- Supported languages
- File size
- Information on privacy; see Examine the app's privacy policies.

Purchase and install an app.

1. Press the pricing button. Tap Get if the app is free.

   If you see a price instead of a download button, you have already purchased the software and can download it for free again.

2. Verify your Apple ID with Face ID, Touch ID, or your passcode if necessary to complete your purchase.

The app can be found under App Library's Recently Added category. A progress indicator appears on the app icon as it is downloading. See On the iPad, look for your apps in the App Library. Change the location where new apps are downloaded.

Download the App Store widget.

On your Home Screen, you can see articles, collections, and in-app events. See On the iPad, you may add widgets.

Give or share an app.

1. To access the app's details, tap it.
2. Tap, then select a sharing option or gift an app (not available for all apps).

Apple Gift Cards can be redeemed or sent.

1. At the upper right, tap or your profile image.
2. Select one of the following options:
- Use a Gift Card or a Code to Redeem
- You can send a gift card by email.

iPad games to play

You can find your next game in hundreds of categories in the App Store app, including action, adventure, racing, puzzles, and more. You may also use Game Center to play with your friends, collect achievements, and compete on leaderboards.

Note: that not all countries or areas have Game Center, Apple Arcade, or Apple One. See the Apple Support article for further information. Apple Media Services are available. Apple Arcade games are available on a variety of devices, depending on hardware and software compatibility. It's possible that certain content isn't available in all places. See the Apple Support article for further information. Apple Arcade games are available on all Apple devices.

Look for and download games.

1. Select one of the following options:
- Games: See what's new, check out the top charts, or browse by category.
- Arcade: Play Apple Arcade's curated library of premium games without commercials or in-app purchases (membership required).
- Search: Type in what you're looking for and then press the Search key on your keyboard.
2. Select one of the following options to download a game:
- The cost: Purchase the game.

If you see a download button instead of a price, you have previously purchased the game and can download it for free again.

- Obtain: The game is available for free or as part of an Apple Arcade membership. You'll be notified when the game becomes available if it's coming soon.
3. Verify your Apple ID using Face ID, Touch ID, or your passcode if necessary.

Use your other Apple devices to play Apple Arcade games. If you have an Apple Arcade subscription, you can play and track your game progress on compatible Apple devices using your Apple ID. (Not all Apple Arcade games are compatible with the Mac or Apple TV.) All of your Apple Arcade gaming data is accessible across all of your devices.

Connect an iPad to a wireless game controller.

Consult the instructions provided by the manufacturer. On the iPad, set up and use Bluetooth accessories.

In Game Center, you can play with your pals. With Game Center, you can issue friend invites, manage your public profile, and track your high scores across all of your Apple devices.

1. Sign in with your Apple ID by going to Settings > Game Center.
2. Select one of the following options to create a Game Center profile:

- Pick a nickname: Tap Nickname, then type or select a name from the drop-down menu. When you play games with your pals, they will see your nickname.
- Customize your profile picture by tapping Edit at the top, then creating a new Memoji, using an existing Memoji, or changing the appearance of your initials.

3. To invite someone from your Contacts list, hit Add Friends, then input their phone number or Apple ID, or tap to invite someone from your Contacts list.
4. Friendship requests can be responded to in one of the following ways:

- Tap the link under Messages.

- Tap the Game Center profile image, then Friends, then Friend Requests in a compatible game.
- Tap or your profile image in the top right corner of the App Store, then Game Center, then Friend Requests.

Tap a buddy in your list of friends to discover what games they've recently played and their achievements. You can also report a person for cheating, having an improper photo or nickname, or for any other issue. Tap Remove Friend to get rid of a friend.

Place limits on Game Center.

You can restrict multiplayer gaming, adding friends, private chat, and other features.

1. Turn on Content & Privacy Restrictions in Settings > Screen Time > Content & Privacy Restrictions.
2. Go to Content Limitations, scroll down to Game Center, and set the restrictions there.

Apple Arcade is available on iPad as a subscription service. You may subscribe to Apple Arcade in the App

Store app to get unlimited access to a handpicked range of games on your iPhone, iPad, iPod touch, Mac, and Apple TV. (Not all Apple Arcade games are compatible with the Mac or Apple TV.) Apple Arcade can be purchased alone or as part of Apple One, which includes Apple Arcade as well as other services. See the Apple Support article for further information. Apple subscriptions can be combined with Apple One.

It's worth noting that Apple Arcade and Apple One aren't available in every country or region. See the Apple Support article Apple Media Services Availability for more information. Apple Arcade games are available on a variety of devices, depending on hardware and software compatibility. It's possible that certain content isn't available in all places. Apple

Arcade game availability across devices may be seen in the Apple Support article.

Apple Arcade subscription service.

1. Open the App Store and go to Arcade, then to Subscriptions.
2. Review the free trial and membership information (if applicable), then follow the onscreen instructions.

You may change or cancel your Apple Arcade subscription at any time.

Follow the onscreen instructions by going to Settings > [your name] > Subscriptions, tapping Apple Arcade, and then following the onscreen steps.

You won't be able to play any Apple Arcade games if you cancel your subscription, even if you have them downloaded on your device. If you don't want the apps anymore, delete them. You can resubscribe to Apple Arcade games and recover access to your saved game data by doing so. If you wait too long to resubscribe, some of your gaming data may not be maintained.

Share Apple Arcade with your friends and family.

You can utilize Family Sharing to share Apple Arcade with up to five other family members when you subscribe to Apple Arcade or Apple One. Your family members won't have to do anything because Apple Arcade will be available the first time they open the App Store app when your subscription starts.

If you join an Apple Arcade or Apple One family group and already have a subscription, your subscription will not be renewed on your next billing date; instead, you will use the group's subscription. If you join a family group that does not subscribe, your subscription is used by the group.

Note: To stop sharing Apple Arcade with a family group, you can cancel your subscription, leave the family group, or stop using Family Sharing (if you're the family group administrator). On the iPad, use App Clips. An App Clip is a brief section of an app that allows you to rapidly complete a job, such as renting a bike, paying for parking, or ordering meals. App Clips can be found in Safari, Maps, and Messages, as well as in the real world via QR codes and App Clip Codes, which are unique markers that lead to specific App Clips.

Get an App Clip and put it to good use.

1. Choose an App Clip from one of the following options:

- Scan the app clip code or QR code using the iPad camera or the Code Scanner in Control Center (not supported on iPad Air 2 or iPad mini 4).
- Maps: On the information card, tap the App Clip link (for supported locations).
- Tap the App Clip link in Safari or Messages.

2. Tap Open or Play when the App Clip displays on the screen.

Sign in with Apple and then make a payment with Apple Pay in supported App Clips. You may see the whole app by tapping the banner at the top of the screen with several App Clips.

Locate an iPad App Clip that you previously utilized.

Go to App Library, type something in the search area at the top of the screen, and scroll down to the alphabetical list's conclusion.

App Clips should be removed.

- Uninstall a certain App Clip: Go to App Library, hit the search area at the top of the screen, type the App Clip's name, and then tap and hold the app icon.

- Get rid of all app clips: To access App Clips, go to Settings > App Clips.

On iPad, you can manage your App Store purchases, subscriptions, settings, and limits.

You may manage subscriptions, as well as review and download purchases made by you or other family members, through the App Store app. In Settings, you may also set limitations and adjust your App Store preferences. With Family Sharing, you can approve purchases.

The family organizer can evaluate and authorize purchases made by other family members under a specific age when Family Sharing is enabled. Locate and download apps that you or your family members have purchased.

1. At the top right of your screen, press on your profile image, then tap Purchased.
2. If Family Sharing is enabled, tap My Purchases or select a family member to see their purchases.

Note that you will only be able to see purchases made by family members if they opt to share their purchases with you. Purchases made through Family Sharing may be inaccessible once a family member quits the group.

3. Locate and tap the app you want to download (if it's still accessible in the App Store).

Your App Store subscriptions can be changed or cancelled.

1. Go to the top right of your screen and hit on your profile image, then tap Subscriptions.

It's possible that you'll have to check in using your Apple ID.

2. Select a subscription, then choose one of the following options:
- Modify or cancel a current subscription.
- Renew a subscription that has already expired.
- In your Family Sharing group, share an applicable App Store subscription with other family members.

Modify your App Store preferences.

Go to Settings > App Store and perform one of the following actions:

- Download apps purchased on other Apple devices automatically: Turn on Apps under Automatic Downloads.
- Update apps automatically: Activate App Updates.
- Allow cellular data to be used for app downloads (Wi-Fi + Cellular models) Turn on Automatic Downloads under Cellular Data. Tap App Downloads to select whether you want to be asked for permission for downloads larger than 200 MB or for all apps.
- Play app preview videos automatically: Activate the video autoplay feature.
- Delete unneeded apps automatically: Offload Unused Apps should be enabled. If an app is still accessible in the App Store, you can reinstall it at any time.

Set content limits and disable in-app purchases.

Do the following after you've enabled content and privacy restrictions.

1. Go to Screen Time > Content & Privacy Restrictions > Content Restrictions in Settings

> Screen Time > Content & Privacy Restrictions > Content Restrictions.

2. Put limitations in place, such as the following:

- Apps: Set age limits for apps.
- App Clips: Disable the opening of App Clips.

Fonts may be installed and managed on the iPad. Fonts can be downloaded via the App Store app and then used in documents created on the iPad.

1. Open an app containing fonts that you downloaded from the App Store to install the fonts.
2. Go to Settings > General, then Fonts to manage installed fonts.

Apple Books for iPad allows you to purchase books and audiobooks. You can find today's bestsellers, check top rankings, and explore lists created by Apple Books editors in the Books app. You can read or listen to a book or audiobook straight in the app after you've chosen one.

1. Tap Books, then Book Store or Audiobooks to explore titles, or Search to find a certain title, author, or genre.

2. Tap a book cover to learn more about it, read a sample, listen to a preview, or add it to your collection of books to read.

3. To purchase a title, press Buy, or to obtain a free title, tap Get.

The payment method linked with your Apple ID is used for all purchases. You can allow books and audiobooks to be downloaded automatically over your cellular network when you aren't connected to Wi-Fi on iPad models that connect to a cellular network. Scroll to Cellular Data, tap Downloads, and then tap Always Allow in Settings > Books.

Use the Reading Now and Library tabs at the bottom of the screen in the Books app to see what you're reading now, what you plan to read later, your book collections, and more.

- Currently Reading: To access the books and audiobooks you're reading right now, tap. Scroll down to discover what books and audiobooks you've added to you Want to Read list, as well as what books you've tried out. You can also establish daily reading goals and keep track of how many books you read each year.

- Library: Tap to see all of the books, audiobooks, series, and PDFs you've added to your library manually or via the Book Store. Get a book and read it.

To open a book, tap Reading Now or Library, then select a cover. To navigate, use the following motions and controls:

- To turn the page, swipe right to left or tap the right side of the page.
- Return to the previous page by clicking here: Swipe left to right or tap the left side of the page.
- To get to a certain page, tap it and swipe left or right with the slider at the bottom of the screen. Alternatively, tap and input a page number, then tap it in the search results.
- Put a book down: To reveal the controls, tap the page's middle, then tap.

Tip: To view two pages at once, rotate your iPad to landscape mode.

Personalized recommendations display when you complete a book to help you find your next read.

Text and display appearance can be changed.

Tap the page, then tap one of the options below:

- Change the brightness of the screen: Slide the slider to the left or right.
- Change the font size by tapping the large A or the small A to raise or reduce the font size.
- Change the typeface: Go to Fonts and select a new font.
- Change the color of the page's background: Make a circle with your finger.
- •When the room is dark, dim the screen: When using Books in low-light conditions, turn on Auto-Night Theme to automatically alter the page color and brightness. (Auto-Night Theme isn't supported by all books.)
- Disable pagination: To scroll constantly through a book or PDF, enable Vertical Scrolling.

Make a note of a page.

You don't need to add a bookmark to save your place in a book when you close it. Make a note of pages you'd like to revisit. To add a bookmark, tap it once, then tap it again to remove it. To see all of your bookmarks, go to and select Bookmarks.

Text can be highlighted or underlined.

1. Select a word by touching and holding it, then adjusting the selection by moving the grab points.
2. Select a highlight color or underlining by tapping Highlight.

Tap the text, then tap to remove a highlight or underlining. Tap, then Notes to see all of your highlights.

Make a note of it

1. Select a word by touching and holding it, then adjusting the selection by moving the grab points.
2. Tap Note, then type your message.
3. To close the message and continue reading, tap the page.

Tap, then Notes to see all of your notes. To erase a note, swipe left on it.

Make a selection and share it.

Text selections can be sent via Airdrop, Mail, or Messages, or they can be saved in Notes. If the book is from the Book Store, the selection includes a link to the book. (Not all countries or regions have sharing capabilities.)

1. Select a word by touching and holding it, then adjusting the selection by moving the grab points.
2. Select a method from the Share menu.
1. You may also send a link to the Book Store where the book can be seen. Tap a page, then tap and then tap again.

All of your devices will be able to access your books.

Sign in with the same Apple ID on each device to keep your Books information up to current, then do the following:

- Sync the position of the book, bookmarks, notes, and highlights: Turn on both iCloud Drive and Books in Settings > [your name] > iCloud.
- To sync Reading Now, Library, and Collections, go to Settings > [your name] > iCloud and enable both iCloud Drive and Books. Then go to Settings > Books and select Reading Now from the drop-down menu.

On your Mac, you may access your books.

Choose Apple menu > System Preferences, then one of the following options to see your books, audiobooks, and PDFs on your Mac:

- macOS 10.15 or later: Go to System Preferences, pick Apple ID, then iCloud in the sidebar, then iCloud Drive. Select Books from the drop-down menu under Options.
- If you're using macOS 10.14 or before, go to System Preferences, then iCloud, then iCloud Drive. Select Books from the drop-down menu under Options.

Calendar on iPad allows you to create and edit events.

Create and edit events, appointments, and meetings with the Calendar App. Say something like, "Set up a meeting with Gordon at 9 a.m." or "Do I have a meeting at 10 a.m." to Siri.

Create a new event.

1. Tap the top of the screen in day view.
2. Type in the event's name.
3. Select Location or Video Call, then input a physical address or FaceTime to create a video link for a remote meeting.

You can also paste a FaceTime link that you made or received in the Location area. See Make a link to a FaceTime conversation.

4. Fill in the event's start and end times, travel time, invitees, attachments, and other details. (If necessary, swipe up to enter all of the meeting details.)
5. Press the Add button.

Add a notification

You can set an alert to remind you of an upcoming event.

1. Press the event, then towards the top of the screen, tap Edit.
2. Tap Alert in the event information.
3. Pick a time when you'd like to be reminded.

"At the time of the event," "5 minutes before," or another option. Calendar uses Apple Maps to search up locations, traffic conditions, and transit choices to tell you when it's time to depart if you provide the address of the event's location.

Include a file attachment

You can share an attachment with invitees by adding it to a Calendar event.

1. Tap the event, then Edit in the upper right corner.
2. Tap Add attachment in the event details.
1. The Files app launches, presenting the files you've recently opened.
2. Find the file you'd like to attach.

You can search for the file by typing its name into the search area, scrolling, tapping folders to open them, tapping Browse to seek in other locations (like iCloud Drive), and so on. See Files on iPad allows you to see and modify files and directories.

3. Press the Done button.

To delete the attachment, go to the event, press Edit in the upper right corner, swipe left over the attachment, and then tap Remove.

Other apps can help you find events.

Siri can recommend events from Mail, Messages, and Safari, like as flight reservations and hotel reservations, so you can add them to Calendar quickly.

1. Go to Settings > Calendar > Siri & Search > Siri & Search.
2. Allow Siri to recommend events from other apps by turning on Show Siri Suggestions in App.

Turn on Learn from this App to allow Siri to make suggestions in other apps depending on how you use Calendar.

You can alter the date and time of an event, as well as any other event parameters.

- Adjust the time: Touch and hold an event in day view, then drag it to a new time or alter the grab points.
- Edit event details: Hit the event, select Edit in the top right, then tap a setting to edit it or tap in a field to type new information in the event details.

Delete a specific event

In day view, tap the event, then at the bottom of the screen, press Delete Event.

On the iPad, you may personalize your calendar.

You may choose the day of the week Calendar starts on, display week numbers, select alternate calendars (for example, Chinese or Hebrew dates), override the default time zone, and more in the Calendar app.

Go to Settings > Calendar, then select the desired settings and features.

On the iPad, you may share iCloud calendars.

You may share an iCloud calendar with other iCloud users using the Calendar app. Others can view your calendar when you share it, and you can allow them to add or change events. You can also share a read-only version with anyone who wants to look at it but not edit it.

Make a calendar in iCloud.

1. Press the button.
2. Select Add Calendar.
3. Give the new calendar a name, then hit Done.

An iCloud calendar can be shared.

In iCloud, you can share a calendar with one or more individuals. Your invitees will be sent an invitation to join the calendar.

1. Press the button.
2. Tap the iCloud calendar you'd like to share.

3. Tap Add Person, then type in a name or email address, or swipe through your Contacts.

4. Select Add.

Change the permissions on a shared calendar for a specific individual. After inviting someone to share your calendar, you can enable or disable their ability to edit it, as well as cease sharing the calendar with them.

1. Tap, then tap the person next to the shared calendar.

2. Carry out one of the following actions:

- Activate or deactivate Allow Editing.

- Press the Stop Sharing button.

Disable calendar notifications for shared calendars.

When someone makes an update to a calendar you're sharing, you'll be notified. If you don't want to receive notifications for shared calendars, you can turn them off.

1. Select Settings > Notifications > Calendar > Shared Calendar Changes from the drop-down menu.

1. Allow Notifications should be turned off.

2. Anyone can view a read-only calendar.

forecast for today?" "Hey Siri, set an alarm for 8 a.m."
or "Hey Siri, set an alarm for 8 a.m."

1. Say "Hey Siri" or tap to ask Siri another inquiry
   or perform another action.

Place your iPad face down to prevent it from
responding to "Hey Siri," or click to Settings > Siri &
Search, then turn off Listen for "Hey Siri."

While wearing supporting AirPods, you can also
activate Siri by saying "Hey Siri." In the AirPods User
Guide, go to Set up Siri.

Siri is activated by pressing a button.

Siri answers silently when you engage Siri with a
button while the iPad is silenced. Change how Siri
reacts to learn how to do so.

1. Complete one of the following tasks:
- Press and hold the Home button on an iPad with
  a Home button.
- Press and hold the top button on other iPad
  models.
- EarPods with Mic and Remote: (Sold separately)
  Hold the center or call button down.

2. When Siri appears, ask her a question or request that she complete a task for you.

For instance, "What is 18 percent of 225?" or "Set the timer for three minutes."

3. Tap to ask Siri a new question or complete a task.

With supporting AirPods, you can also activate Siri with a touch. In the AirPods User Guide, go to Set Up Siri.

If Siri misunderstands you, correct it.

- Rephrase your request as follows: Then tap and say your request in a new way.
- Specify a portion of your request: Tap and then rephrase your request, spelling out any terms Siri didn't comprehend the first time. Say, "Call," and then spell the person's name.
- Before sending a message, make changes to it: "Change it," you say.
- Add text to your request: You can make changes to your request if you see it onscreen. Then, using the onscreen keyboard, tap the request.

Instead of speaking to Siri, type.

1. Go to Settings > Accessibility > Siri, then select Type to Siri from the drop-down menu.
2. To make a request, open Siri and use the keyboard and text box to ask Siri a question or have Siri perform a task for you.

If Siri on your iPad isn't working as it should, check out this Apple Support post. If "Hey Siri" on your iPhone or iPad isn't working. Siri is meant to keep your information safe, and you have complete control over what you share. See the Ask Siri, Dictation & Privacy website for additional information.

See what Siri can do on the iPad.

On the iPad, use Siri to receive information and complete tasks. Siri and its responses appear on top of whatever you're doing right now, allowing you to refer to information displayed onscreen. Siri is a conversationalist. You can tap a web link displayed by Siri to access more information in your default web browser. You can tap the buttons or controls shown in Siri's onscreen response to take additional action. You can also ask Siri a new question or have her perform a new activity for you. Here are some examples of what

Siri can do for you. Additional examples can be found throughout the book. You may also ask Siri the following questions: "Hey Siri, what can you do?" you might say.

Answer queries with Siri.

Use Siri to look up information, perform computations, or translate a sentence into another language. "Hey Siri, what produces a rainbow?" you might say.

- "Hey Siri, can you tell me what a cat sounds like?"
- "Hey Siri, what's the cosine x derivative?"
- "Hey Siri, can you tell me how to say Thank You in Mandarin?"

Siri may be used with apps.

Siri allows you to use your voice to operate apps. To establish an event in Calendar, say something like: "Hey Siri, set up a meeting with Gordon at 9 a.m."

- To add an item to Reminders, say "Hey Siri, add artichokes to my groceries list."
- Say, "Hey Siri, what's my update?" to get information on the weather in your location, the

news, your reminders and calendar events, and other topics.

See any of the following for further examples:

- Use Siri on iPad to announce calls, messages, and more.
- On the iPad, use Siri to play music and listen to music with Apple Music Voice.
- Use Siri on your iPad to control your home.
- Get directions on the iPad with Siri, Maps, and the Maps widget.
- On the iPad, enable Siri Shortcuts

To communicate information with contacts, use Siri.

With people in your contacts, you may share onscreen items like images, webpages, content from Apple Music or Apple Podcasts, Maps locations, and more.

Say something like "Hey Siri, send this to mom" when looking at a photo in your Photo library to compose a new message with the photo.

Siri allows you to customize your experience. The more you use Siri, the better it gets at understanding what you want. You may also provide Siri information about yourself and alter how and when Siri answers. Take a look at any of the following:

- iPad Siri Suggestions
- On the iPad, tell Siri about yourself.
- On the iPad, change the Siri settings.

You may also use Siri's accessibility features.

Siri is meant to keep your information safe, and you have complete control over what you share. See the Ask Siri, Dictation & Privacy website for additional information.

On the iPad, tell Siri about yourself.

For a more personalized experience, you may equip Siri with information such as your home and work addresses, as well as your relationships, so you can say things like "Give me driving instructions home" and "FaceTime mom."

Let Siri know who you are.

1. Go to Contacts and enter your contact information.
2. Tap your name after going to Settings > Siri & Search > My Information.

Inform Siri about a romantic relationship.

"Hey Siri, Eliza Block is my wife," or "Hey Siri, Ashley Kamin is my mother," for example. On your Apple devices, keep up to speed with what Siri knows about you. Go to Settings on each device and sign in with the same Apple ID. If you utilize iCloud, end-to-end encryption keeps your Siri settings up to date across all of your Apple devices. You may disable Siri in iCloud settings if you don't want your Siri personalization to sync across your iPad and other devices. Turn off Siri by going to Settings > [your name] > iCloud.

Note: If you have Location Services enabled on your device, Apple receives the location of your device at the time you make a request to help Siri and Dictation enhance the accuracy of their responses to your requests. Apple may utilize your internet connection's IP address to approximate your location by matching it to a geographic region in order to give relevant responses. See Control the information you share about your location on your iPad. Siri on iPad can be used to announce phone calls, messages, and more.

On approved headphones, Siri can announce calls and notifications from apps like Messages. You can use your voice to answer or respond without saying "Hey Siri." Announce Calls and Announce Notifications are also compatible with third-party apps that are supported.

Allow Siri to make phone calls.

Siri recognizes incoming FaceTime calls and lets you accept or decline them using your voice using Announce Calls.

1. Select an option from Settings > Siri & Search > Announce Calls.
2. When you receive a call, Siri recognizes the caller and asks if you want to answer it. Accept or decline the call by saying "yes" or "no."

Allow Siri to read out notifications.

Siri can announce incoming notifications from apps like Messages and Reminders automatically. For apps that employ time-sensitive notifications, Siri automatically enables app notifications, but you may adjust the settings at any time. Set up a Focus on iPad to learn more about time-sensitive notifications.

1. Turn on Announce Notifications in Settings > Siri & Search > Announce Notifications.

2. Select an app from which you want Siri to announce alerts, then select Announce Notifications from the drop-down menu.

You can also choose whether or not to announce all notifications or only time-sensitive notifications for particular apps. Siri repeats what you said before asking for confirmation before sending your reply in apps where you can send a reply, such as Messages. Turn on Reply Without Confirmation to send replies without waiting for confirmation.

Shortcuts for Siri on iPad

Some programs provide shortcuts for tasks that you perform regularly. These shortcuts can be activated just by speaking to Siri. For instance, a travel app may allow you to view your upcoming journey event simply by asking Siri, "Where am I heading next?"

Add a recommended shortcut.

When you see a shortcut suggestion, tap Add to Siri, then follow the onscreen instructions to record a phrase that performs the shortcut.

The Shortcuts app also allows you to create new Siri shortcuts, as well as manage, re-record, and delete current Siri shortcuts. See the Shortcuts User Guide for further information.

Make use of a shortcut.

Activate Siri, then speak your shortcut phrase. See On the iPad, ask Siri a question.

Siri also provides shortcuts on the Home Screen, Lock Screen, and when you start a search based on your routines and how you use your apps. Change Siri settings for a specific app to turn off shortcut suggestions for that app.

iPad Siri Suggestions

Based on your routines and how you use your apps, Siri suggests what you might want to do next, such as confirm an appointment or send an email. For instance, Siri might come in handy if you're doing any of the following:

- Look at the Lock Screen or start a search: As Siri gets to know your habits, you'll get suggestions for exactly what you're looking for, at exactly the right time.
- Create emails and events: When you begin adding people to an email or calendar event, Siri

suggests people you've previously included in emails or activities.

- Leave for an event: If your calendar event specifies a location, Siri evaluates traffic conditions and alerts you when it's time to depart.
- Type: As you type, Siri will recommend movie titles, locations, and anything else you've lately seen on your iPad. If you tell a friend you're on your way, Siri will even give you an estimate of when you'll arrive.
- Search in Safari: As you write in the search bar, Siri provides websites and other information.
- (Apple iPad Air 2 and newer) Siri also proposes words and phrases depending on what you've just read above the keyboard.
- Read news stories: (iPad Air 2 and later) Siri asks if you want to add it to your calendar when you confirm an appointment or book a trip on a travel website. Siri will propose things you're interested in as you learn more about them.

Change Siri settings on iPad to change the settings for Siri Suggestions.

Your personal information, which is encrypted and kept private, is synced across all of your devices if you use the same Apple ID. As Siri learns more about you on one device, your overall experience with Siri improves. You may disable Siri in iCloud settings if you don't want your Siri customization to update across all of your devices. See On your Apple devices, keep up to speed with what Siri knows about you.

Siri is meant to keep your information safe, and you have complete control over what you share. Visit the Siri Suggestions, Search, and Privacy website to learn more.

On the iPad, change the Siri settings.

You may modify Siri's voice, prohibit Siri from accessing your smartphone when it's locked, and more.When Siri responds, change it.

Go to Settings > Siri & Search, then select one of the options below:

- Stop Siri from responding to "Hey Siri" voice commands: Turn off the "Hey Siri" feature.
- Stop Siri from reacting when you press the Home or Top buttons: Press Home for Siri (on an iPad

with a Home button) or Press Top Button for Siri (on an iPad without a Home button) (on other iPad models).

- When the iPad is locked, prevent access to Siri: When your phone is locked, turn off Allow Siri.
- Modify Siri's response language: Select a new language by tapping Language.

Siri can also be activated by typing. See Instead of speaking to Siri, type.

Modify Siri's responses.

Go to Settings > Siri & Search, then select one of the options below:

- For Siri, change the voice: (not available in all languages) Choose a different kind or voice by tapping Siri Voice.
- Alter the timing of Siri's voice responses: Select an option underneath Spoken Responses after tapping Siri Responses.
- Siri's response is always visible onscreen: Turn on Always Show Siri Captions after tapping Siri Responses.

- Look at your request on the screen: Turn on Always Show Speech after tapping Siri Responses.

- When you activate Siri, hide your apps.

Go to Settings > Accessibility > Siri, then turn off Show Apps Behind Siri if you don't want the active app to be visible behind Siri.

Change the location of Siri's suggestions.

Go to Settings > Siri & Search, then toggle any of the following options on or off:

- Make Notifications Available
- Display in App Library and Spotlight
- Display When Sharing
- Display When Listening

CHAPTER EIGHT

FAMILY SHARING

Family members can share purchases, subscriptions, their location, and more without having to exchange accounts when you set up Family Sharing. For children, you may also set up parental controls. One adult member of the family, the organizer, forms a family sharing group and asks up to five other family members to join. When family members join, they get immediate access to the content that has been provided.

Make a group for family sharing.

Only one device needs to be set up for Family Sharing. Then it'll be available on all of your devices that share the same Apple ID.

1. Go to Settings ⚙ > [your name] > Family Sharing, then set up your Family Sharing group by following the onscreen steps.

You can designate an adult family member as a parent or guardian when you add them. Learn about the many types of members who make up a Family Sharing group.

2. Select a feature for your Family Sharing group, then follow the on-screen instructions.

You may be required to set up a subscription depending on the options you select. You agree to pay for any purchases your family members make while in the Family Sharing group if you choose to share App Store, music, movie, TV, and book purchases with them. Adults and teenagers in the household can disable buy sharing for themselves. You can always view what you're sharing with your family and change your sharing settings. Features you've shared with your family are prioritized over those you haven't.

What Can Family Sharing Be Used for?

You can set up or share the following with a Family Sharing group:

- Apple and App Store subscriptions: You can share qualifying App Store subscriptions and Apple subscriptions, including iCloud+. On the iPad, go to Share Apple and App Store subscriptions with family members.
- Purchases: You can share purchases from the iTunes Store, App Store, Apple Books, and Apple TV. See Download purchases made by family members to your iPad.
- Locations: When you share your location with family members, they can use the Find My app to see where you are and assist in the recovery of a lost device.
- Apple Card and Apple Cash: You can share Apple Card with trustworthy family members or create an Apple Cash Family account for a child. See On the iPad, use Apple Cash and Apple Card with Family Sharing (U.S. only).

- Parental controls: Manage your children's purchases and how they use their Apple devices using parental controls. See Set up parental controls on the iPad using Family Sharing.

On the iPad, you can add or remove members from your Family Sharing group. The organizer of a Family Sharing group can add family members who have an Apple ID. A youngster can be added to the group and given an Apple ID by the organizer, a parent, or a guardian. Family members who aren't teens with parental controls or children can opt out or the group can be disbanded, and family members who aren't teens with parental controls or children can opt out. If you remove children from your group or disband it, they must be reassigned to another Family Sharing group. See the Apple Support article for further information. Using Family Sharing, move a child to a different group.

Add a member of your family who has an Apple ID.

The Family Sharing group's organizer can add a family member who has their own Apple ID.

1. Tap Add Member under Settings > [your name] > Family Sharing.
2. Tap Invite People, then follow the directions on the screen.

You can use AirDrop, Messages, or Mail to send the invitation. If you're in close proximity to the family member, hit Invite in Person and ask them to input their Apple ID and password on your iPhone.

How to create an Apple ID.

If a child is too young to create an Apple ID on their own, the organizer, a parent, or a guardian can add the child to the Family Sharing group and create an Apple ID on their behalf.

1. Go to [your name] > Settings > Family Sharing.
2. If you're the organizer, press Add Member, then tap Create an Account for a Child, and then follow the onscreen instructions.
- If you're a parent or guardian, tap Add Child and then follow the onscreen prompts.

See the Apple Support article for more information on kid accounts and the age at which a child can create their own Apple ID. For your youngster, create an Apple ID.

How to remove a family member from a group.

Other members of a Family Sharing group can be removed by the group's organizer. When a member of the family is removed, they lose access to any shared content and subscriptions right away.

1. Go to [your name] > Settings > Family Sharing.
2. Tap Remove [member's name] from Family, then tap [member's name].

You cease sharing your purchases and memberships with family members when you leave a Family Sharing group, and you lose immediate access to any content they've shared. The organizer is not permitted to quit the Family Sharing group. You must disband the group and have another adult form a new one if you want to alter the organizer.

1. Go to [your name] > Settings > Family Sharing.
2. Tap [your name], then tap Stop Using Family Sharing to exit the app.

A Family Sharing group should be disbanded.

A family group can be disbanded by the organizer. When a Family Sharing group is broken up, all members lose access to the shared content and subscriptions right away.

1. Go to [your name] > Family Sharing > [your name] > Settings > [your name].
2. Select Stop Using Family Sharing from the drop-down menu.

On the iPad, you may share Apple and App Store subscriptions with family members. You can share Apple subscriptions and qualified App Store subscriptions with other family members if you're a member of a Family Sharing group. If purchase sharing is enabled in your Family Sharing group, any subscriptions shared with the group will be invoiced to the organizer's Apple ID account. Some selections are subject to content limitations established under Screen Time, and not all services are available in all countries or areas.

Subscriptions to Apple can be shared.

1. Go to [your name] > Settings > Family Sharing.

2. Select a subscription and follow the onscreen prompts.

- Apple Arcade: For further information, see Subscribe to Apple Arcade on iPad. From the App Store, all members of your family can download and play Apple Arcade games. Each player is given a unique account, and your progress is synced between devices.

- Apple Fitness+: The Apple Watch User Guide has all you need to know about Apple Fitness+. Your entire family can use the Fitness app on their iPhone or iPad to do workouts.

- Apple Music: See Subscribe to Apple Music on iPad for further information. Each family member gets their own music collection and personalized recommendations with a family subscription.

- Apple News+: See Subscribe to Apple News+ on iPad for more information. Apple News+ publications are available to all members of your family at no additional cost.

- Apple TV+ and Apple TV channels: See Apple TV+ on iPad and Apple TV Channels. On the iPad, set up the Apple TV app. Using their own Apple ID and password, each family member may watch on their iPhone, iPad, iPod touch, Mac, Apple TV, and supported smart TVs and streaming devices.

- iCloud+: See Subscribe to iCloud+ on iPad for more information. All family members have access to iCloud+ features and storage when you share iCloud+. You merely share the storage space; your photos and papers remain private, and everyone maintains their own accounts.

See the Apple Support article for more information on combining your Apple memberships. Apple subscriptions can be combined with Apple One.

Subscriptions to the App Store can be shared.

You have the option of sharing which applicable App Store subscriptions with family members. See Get apps in the App Store on iPad for more information about the App Store.

1. Go to [your name] > Settings > Subscriptions.
2. Choose one of the following options:
3. Distribute any new subscriptions: Turn on the option to share new subscriptions. When you buy a new membership that is qualified for sharing,

it is automatically shared with your family members.

4. Modify the preferences for a specific subscription: Turn Share with Family on or off by tapping a subscription.

If Share with Family isn't available, your subscription isn't qualified for sharing.

Go to Settings > [your name] > Family Sharing to discover which subscriptions you've previously shared.

You can also share purchases made on the iTunes Store, App Store, Apple Books, and Apple TV with your family. See Download purchases made by family members to your iPad. Purchases made by family members can be downloaded on an iPad.

You and up to five family members can share iTunes Store, App Store, Apple Books, and Apple TV purchases when you set up Family Sharing.

All App Store, music, movie, TV, and book purchases made by your family are billed to the family organizer's Apple ID account. Adults and teenagers in the household can disable buy sharing for themselves. The family organizer can also require that purchases or free downloads be approved by the youngsters in the family group. See Set up parental controls on the iPad using Family Sharing.

Once purchased, the item is placed to the account of the initiating family member, and qualified purchases are shared with the rest of the family.

1. Go to the iTunes Store and select Purchased.
2. Pick a member of your family.
3. At the top of the screen, select a category (for example, Music), then tap a purchased item, then tap.

On the iPad, see Manage your iTunes Store purchases and preferences.

From the App Store, download shared purchases.

1. Go to the App Store and download the app.
2. At the top right, tap —or your profile image.
3. Tap Purchased, then select a family member before tapping.

On iPad, you may also manage App Store purchases, subscriptions, settings, and limits.

Apple Books allows you to download shared purchases.

1. Launch the Books app.

2. In the top right corner, tap or your profile image.

3. Tap a category, then tap the name of a family member under Family Purchases (for example, Books or Audiobooks).

4. Tap All, Recent Purchases, or a genre, then tap the download icon next to a purchased item.

On the iPad, you can also buy books and audiobooks through Apple Books.

From the Apple TV app, you can download shared purchases.

1. Launch the Apple TV application.

2. Tap Family Sharing in the sidebar under the Library header, then select a family member.

3. Tap a genre or a category (for example, TV Shows or Movies), then tap to download a purchased item.

1. On the iPad, see Manage your library in the Apple TV app.

On the iPad, use Apple Cash and Apple Card with Family Sharing (U.S. only)

Apple Cash can be set up for a child by the Family Sharing group's organizer. They can also share Apple Card with their Family Sharing group's trustworthy members. Learn about the many types of members who make up a Family Sharing group.

Create an Apple Cash Family account.

Apple Cash Family can be set up in Family Sharing settings by the family organizer so that Apple Cash can be set up for a child.

1. Go to [your name] > Settings > Family Sharing.
2. Select Apple Cash and then follow the onscreen prompts.

The family organizer may check the card balance, monitor transactions, and limit who the youngster can send money to by going to Settings > Wallet & Apple Pay. See Maintain control over your Apple Cash.

See the Apple Support article for more information on system requirements and how to manage Apple Cash accounts. Apple Cash Family is simple to set up and use.

Create an Apple Card Family account.

The family organizer can ask one 18-year-old or older member of their Family Sharing group to co-own Apple Card. Participants must be 13 years old or older to be added to the Family Sharing group.

1. Go to Settings > Wallet & Apple Pay > Apple Card, then press it.
2. Tap Share My Card, then follow the directions on the screen.

The organizer can set up parental controls for children in the Family Sharing group using Family Sharing. Screen Time allows you to control how your children use their Apple products. You can also enable Ask to Buy, which requires parental approval before purchases or free downloads are made.

Set aside time for a child to watch television.

You can adjust settings for downtime, app use allowances, the people your child communicates with, content ratings, and more when you set up Screen Time for a child. Your child must be using an eligible device to participate in Screen Time.

1. Go to [your name] > Family Sharing > Screen Time in Settings.
2. Hit a family member's name, then tap Turn on Screen Time and follow the onscreen instructions.

Important: You can reset the family Screen Time passcode if you set up Screen Time for a child with Family Sharing and forget it. See the Apple Support article for further information. If you've forgotten your Screen Time passcode, don't worry. When you set up Ask to Buy, the family organizer or a parent or adult in the family group must approve a child's purchases.

1. Go to [your name] > Settings > Family Sharing.
2. Tap Ask to Buy, then choose one of the options below:

- If your family group doesn't have any children, tap Add Child or Create a Child Account, then follow the onscreen instructions.
- If your family group includes a youngster, tap the child's name, then turn on Ask to Buy.

CHAPTER NINE

SCREEN TIME

Screen Time can help you learn more about how you and your family spend time on their devices, such as which apps and websites you visit, how often you pick up your device, and so on. This data can assist you in making decisions about how to manage your time spent on devices. You may also establish time limits for app use, plan time away from your screen, and more.

Activate Screen Time

Screen Time must be enabled before you can see your app and device usage.

1. Go to Screen Time > Settings.
2. Select Turn On Screen Time and then Select Continue.
3. If you're setting up Screen Time for yourself on your iPad, tap This Is My iPad.

Tap This is My Child's iPad if you're setting up Screen Time for a child (or family member).

4. Scroll down and toggle on Share Across Devices to use Screen Time on all of your Apple devices. If you've set up Family Sharing on your device, you may use it to switch on Screen Time for a family member. See Set up parental controls on the iPad using Family Sharing.

Check out your Screen Time summary.

When you enable Screen Time, you'll be able to get a report of your device usage that includes details like how much time you spend using different types of applications, how often you pick up your iPad and other devices, which apps send you the most notifications, and more.

1. Go to Screen Time > Settings.
2. Tap See All Activity, then Week or Day to see a summary of your weekly or daily usage.

Use the Screen Time widget to keep track of how much time you spend on your devices at a glance. Add a Screen Time widget to your Home Screen to keep track of your device usage from there. The widget displays data from your Screen Time summary; the larger the widget you install; the more data it shows. By glancing at the widget, you may rapidly check your device usage. You can tap the widget to get a list of the people in your family group if you set up Screen Time for them through Family Sharing. To view a report for a family member, tap their name. Screen Time should be used on all of your devices. Make sure you're signed in with the same Apple ID on each device and that Share Across Devices is turned on to share your Screen Time settings and reports across all of your devices.

1. Go to Screen Time > Settings.
2. Go to the bottom of the page and turn on Share Across Devices.

On your iPad, set up Screen Time for yourself.

You may use Screen Time to control your app usage, set aside time away from your gadgets, and more. Any of these settings can be changed or turned off at any time.

Schedule some time away from the computer.

Screen Time allows you to disable apps and notifications for periods of time when you wish to disconnect from your devices. You could wish to arrange breaks between meals or before bedtime, for example.

1. If you haven't already, go to Settings > Screen Time and set it on.
2. Turn on Downtime by tapping Downtime.
3. Choose from Every Day or Customize Days, and then enter the start and stop times.

Turn on downtime whenever you want it.

Only the calls, texts, and apps you choose to enable are available during downtime. During downtime, you can accept calls from contacts you've opted to communicate with, and you can use apps you've chosen to utilize at all times. A five-minute reminder is provided before downtime is switched on when you turn on downtime on demand. If you've planned it, it will stay on until the end of the day or until the start of your scheduled downtime.

1. If you haven't already, go to Settings > Screen Time and set it on.
2. Tap Downtime, then Turn On Downtime Until Tomorrow or Turn On Downtime Until Schedule, as appropriate (if Scheduled is turned on).

Tap Switch Off Downtime to turn off downtime on demand.

Note: You can turn on on-demand downtime for a family member directly on their device or via Family Sharing on your device.

Set app use limitations.

You can set a time restriction for a group of apps (such as Games or Social Networking) as well as for individual apps.

1. If you haven't already, go to Settings > Screen Time and set it on.
2. Go to App Limits and then Add Limit.
3. Choose one or more app categories from the drop-down menu.

To establish individual app limitations, press the category name to see all of the apps in that category, then pick the apps you want to restrict. If you choose multiple categories or apps, the time limit you choose will apply to them all.

4. Tap Next, then enter the amount of time you want to allow.

Tap Customize Days, then set restrictions for certain days to select an amount of time for each day.

5. When you're done with the limitations, press Add.
   On the App Constraints screen, tap App Limits to temporarily disable all app limits. To turn off a

time limit for a specific category temporarily, tap the category and then turn off App Limit.

Set communication limits for a category by tapping the category, then deleting the limit. You can choose to enable or prohibit communication from selected iCloud contacts at all times or for specific periods of time in Screen Time. This includes incoming and outgoing phone calls, FaceTime calls, and messages.

1. Go to Settings ⚙ > [your name] > iCloud, then turn on Contacts if you haven't already.
2. If you haven't already, go to Settings > Screen Time and set it on.
3. Select one of the following options for communication at all times (other than downtime) by tapping Communication Limits, then tapping During Screen Time.

- Contacts Only: This option allows you to communicate with only your contacts.
- Contacts & Groups with at Least One Contact: To allow one-on-one talks with people in your contacts, as well as group conversations with at least one contact.

- Everyone: Allows you to talk to anyone, including numbers you don't recognize.

4. On the upper left, press Back, then During Downtime. This is already set to the option you chose for During Screen Time. Change this setting to Specific Contacts and then select one of the following options:

- Choose from My Contacts: Select contacts with whom you want to communicate during Downtime.

- Add New Contact: This option allows you to add a person to your contacts list and communicate with them during downtime.

If someone who is currently blocked by your Communication Limit settings tries to call or send you a message, it will be rejected. If you try to call or send a message to someone who is currently blocked by your Communication Limit settings, their name or phone number will appear in red in your list of recent calls or messages, and your communication will fail. When the communication restriction is changed, you can communicate with them. You'll get a Time Limit notification if the limit only applies during downtime.

When the downtime is ended, you can continue communication with the contact.

Change the settings by following the procedures above to resume communication with contacts who have been prohibited by your Communication Limit settings.

Select the apps and contacts you want to have access to at all times. You can set up Screen Time to allow you to utilize apps and chat with contacts at all times—even when you're not working (for example, in the event of an emergency).

1. Select Settings ⊚ > Screen Time > Always Allowed from the drop-down menu.
2. To add or remove an app from the Allowed Apps list, press or next to it below Allowed Apps.
3. Tap Contacts to specify which contacts you want to be able to communicate with.

The Communication Limits option you selected appears here. Change this setting to Specific Contacts and then select one of the following options:

- Pick People from My Contacts: This option allows you to select specific people with whom you want to communicate.

- Add New Contact: This option allows you to add a new contact and communicate with them.

4. At the top left, tap Back.

Establish content and privacy constraints.

You can restrict iTunes Store and App Store purchases and ban unsuitable content.

1. If you haven't already, go to Settings > Screen Time and set it on.

2. Turn on Content & Privacy Restrictions, then touch settings to configure content allowances for iTunes Store and App Store purchases, app use, and content ratings, among other things.

You can also need a passcode before making any changes to the settings.

3. Set content allowances for iTunes Store and App Store purchases, app use, content ratings, and more by selecting options.

Note: On your device (iPadOS 15.1 or later), click to Settings > Screen Time > Content & Privacy Restrictions > Allowed Apps, then turn off SharePlay. **Turn it on to enable SharePlay.**

Set up Screen Time on the iPad for a family member.

Screen Time allows you to monitor how your family members use their devices so you can manage how much time they spend on them. You can set Screen Time for a family member on their device, or you can set Screen Time for a family member on your device if you've enabled Family Sharing. See Set up parental restrictions for your child on the iPad using Family Sharing and the Apple Support Article Family Sharing with Apple ID.

On a family member's device, set downtime and app limits.

1. Go to Settings > Screen Time on your family member's device.
2. Select Turn On Screen Time, Continue, and Then Select This Is My Child's iPad.
3. Enter the start and finish hours, then touch Set Downtime to schedule downtime for your family member (time away from the screen).
4. Select the categories you want to manage (for example, Games or Social Networking) to establish limitations for them.

Tap Show All Categories to show all of the categories.

4. Select Set, input a time limit, and then select Set App Limit.

5. To manage your family member's Screen Time settings, tap Continue, then enter a Screen Time passcode.

Note: You can turn on downtime on demand for a family member directly on their device or through Family Sharing on your device (if Family Sharing is enabled). Set communication restrictions on a family member's phone or tablet.

You can restrict incoming and outgoing communication from particular contacts on your family member's device, including phone calls, FaceTime calls, and messages, at any time or for a specific amount of time.

1. Go to Settings > [child's name] > iCloud, then turn on Contacts if you haven't previously done so on your family member's device.

Note: If your family member uses iCloud Contacts, you can only manage their correspondence.

2. Go to Settings > Screen Time on your family member's device.

3. If you haven't already, press Turn On Screen Time, then tap Continue, then tap Done. This is the iPad that belongs to my child.

4. Select Communication Limits, then choose one of the following options:

- At all times, limit communication: Select Contacts Only, Contacts & Groups with at Least One Contact, or Everyone, then tap During Screen Time.

- Tap During Downtime to limit communication during downtime. This is already set to the option you chose for During Screen Time. This setting can be changed to Specific Contacts.

If you choose Specific Contacts, pick persons you wish to communicate with during downtime by tapping either Choose from My Contacts or Add New Contact.

- Manage a child's contacts: You can manage your child's contacts if you're using Family Sharing. Select Manage [child's name] Contacts from the drop-down menu.

If your child already has contacts in iCloud, a notification will appear on their device asking them to allow the request to manage them. If they don't have any contacts, they won't receive a notification, and you'll be able to add them right away. A new row displays beneath Manage [child's name] Contacts when you manage your child's contacts to show how many contacts they have. By tapping that row, you may view and modify those contacts.

- Allow contact editing: Toggle this option off and prevent your child from editing their contacts, tap Allow Contact Editing.

Turning off contact editing and limiting communication to Contacts Only at any time is a fantastic strategy to regulate who and when your child can communicate with. When someone who is currently blocked by the Communication Limit settings tries to call or message your family member (through phone or FaceTime), their communication will be blocked.

When a member of your family tries to call or send a message to someone who is currently blocked by the Communication Limit settings, the recipient's name or phone number shows in red with a Screen Time hourglass indicator, and the communication fails. If the limit only applies to downtime, your family member will receive a Time Limit notice and will be able to communicate with the contact once the downtime has passed. Change the settings as described above to allow your family member to communicate with contacts who are blocked by the Communication Limit settings. On a family member's device, turn on or off communication safety for messages.

When communication safety is enabled under Screen Time, nudity in images can be recognized in the Messages app before they are transmitted or received by your child, and resources to help them deal with the problem are supplied (U.S. only; iPadOS 15.2 or later). As a result of this feature, Apple does not have access to the images. See the Apple Support article on Messages communication security.

1. Go to Settings > Screen Time on your family member's device.
2. Tap Turn On Screen Time, then Continue, then This is My Child's iPad if you haven't previously done so.

3. Turn on Check for Sensitive Photos under Communication Safety.

Choose which apps to allow on a family member's smartphone at all times.

You can control which apps your family member has access to at any moment.

1. Go to Settings > Screen Time on your family member's device.
2. Tap Turn On Screen Time, then Continue, then This is My Child's iPad if you haven't previously done so.
3. Select Always Allowed from the drop-down menu, then press or next to an app to add or remove it from the list.

Note: If a member of your family requires health or accessibility apps, make sure they're included in the list of Allowed Apps. Your family member may not be able to send or receive messages (including to emergency numbers and contacts) during downtime or after the app limit has elapsed if Messages isn't always authorized. On a family member's device, place content and privacy limitations.

Limiting the explicitness ratings under Content & Privacy Restrictions can assist guarantee that the content on your family member's device is age suitable.

1. Go to Settings > Screen Time on your family member's device.
2. Tap Turn On Screen Time, then Continue, then This is My Child's iPad if you haven't previously done so.
3. Select Content & Privacy Restrictions from the drop-down menu, then enable Content & Privacy Restrictions.
4. Customize your content and privacy settings.

Note: To safeguard your loved one's hearing, scroll down and tap Reduce Loud Sounds, then Don't Allow. (This prevents the maximum headphone volume from being changed.) In Settings, go to Reduce loud headphone sounds.

Note: If you're on iPadOS 15.1 or later, click to Settings > Screen Time > Content & Privacy Restrictions > Allowed Apps, then switch off SharePlay. Turn it on to enable SharePlay.

5. At the top of the screen, tap.

Later, you can add or alter a family member's Screen Time settings. Follow the methods outlined in to add or update Screen Time settings later. On your iPad, set up Screen Time for yourself.

On iPad, get a report on your device usage.

You can get a report on your device usage if you have Screen Time set up.

1. Go to Screen Time > Settings.
2. Tap See All Activity, then select one of the options below:

- Tap Week to receive a summary of your usage for the previous week.
- Tap Day to receive a rundown of your daily activities.
- When a Device Time Weekly Report notice arrives on your screen, you can check your summary by pressing it. (If the notification vanishes, go to Notification Center and look for it.) You may also add a Screen Time widget to your Home Screen to get a quick look at your Screen Time report.

CHAPTER TEN

USE IPAD WITH IPHONE, IPOD TOUCH, MAC, AND PC

Share your iPad's internet connection (Wi-Fi + Cellular). You may use Personal Hotspot to share a cellular internet connection from your iPad (Wi-Fi + Cellular models) to other devices if you have an active cellular data plan. When other devices do not have internet connection through a Wi-Fi network, a Personal Hotspot is useful.

Note: that not all carriers offer Personal Hotspot. There may be additional charges. The number of devices that can connect to your Personal Hotspot at the same time is determined by your iPad model and carrier. For further information, contact your carrier.

Create a personal hotspot on your iPad.

Set up a personal hotspot by going to Settings > Cellular Data, tapping Set Up Personal Hotspot, and then following the onscreen instructions.

Note: If Set Up Personal Hotspot isn't available but you have an active cellular data plan and Cellular Data is enabled in Settings > Cellular Data, contact your carrier about adding Personal Hotspot to your plan.

The following settings can be changed:

- Change your Personal Hotspot's Wi-Fi password: To change your Wi-Fi password, go to Settings > Personal Hotspot > Wi-Fi Password.

- Disconnect devices and turn off Personal Hotspot: Turn off Allow Others to Join in Settings > Personal Hotspot.

- Connect your Personal Hotspot to a Mac or PC.

To connect a Mac or PC to your Personal Hotspot, you can use Wi-Fi, a USB connection, or Bluetooth. Choose one of the following options:

- Connect from a Mac through Wi-Fi: Select your iPad from the list of accessible networks by clicking the Wi-Fi status menu in the menu bar.

Enter the password displayed in Settings > Personal Hotspot on your iPad if prompted.

As long as your Mac is connected to your Personal Hotspot, the Wi-Fi status icon in the menu bar switches to the Personal Hotspot icon.

Note: If your Mac and iPad are both signed in with the same Apple ID and Bluetooth and Wi-Fi are turned on, you can connect your devices to Personal Hotspot without entering a password.

- Connect through Wi-Fi from a computer: Choose your iPad in the Wi-Fi settings on your PC, then enter the password displayed in Settings > Personal Hotspot on your iPad.

- Use a USB cable to connect your iPad to your computer. Tap Trust if you see a message that says "Trust this Computer?" Choose iPad from your computer's network choices, then configure the network settings.

- Use Bluetooth: Go to Settings > Bluetooth and leave the screen visible to ensure that your iPad is discoverable. Then go to Apple menu > System Preferences, click Bluetooth, choose your iPad, and click Connect on a Mac. Tap the name of your Mac on your iPad, and then follow the onscreen instructions on your Mac.

Set up a Bluetooth network connection on a PC by following the manufacturer's instructions. Connect your Personal Hotspot to an iPhone, iPod touch, or another iPad.

Go to Settings > Wi-Fi on the other device, then select your iPad from the list of accessible networks.

If the other device prompts you for a password, enter the one you set in Settings > Personal Hotspot on your iPad.

Note: If you're signed in with the same Apple ID on both devices and Bluetooth and Wi-Fi are turned on, you can connect them without providing a password. A blue band displays at the top of your iPad screen when a device is connected. The Personal Hotspot icon shows in the connected device's status bar. You can share your Personal Hotspot with any member of your family automatically or after they ask for permission via Family Sharing. See Set up iPad Family Sharing.

When you share a Personal Hotspot from your iPad, the internet connection is made using cellular data. Go to

Settings > Cellular Data to keep track of your cellular data consumption. See iPad (Wi-Fi + Cellular models): View or modify cellular data settings.

On the iPad, you may make and receive phone calls.

Using Wi-Fi Calling to relay phone calls through your iPhone, you may make and receive calls on your iPad (iOS 9 or later required). It's possible that you'll be charged for using your phone. Some carriers do not support Wi-Fi Calling.

Important: Wi-Fi + Cellular versions only support cellular data transmission and do not support cellular phone service. Wi-Fi Calling and an iPhone are required to make phone calls on any iPad model.

Before you start, make sure you have everything you need.

Perform the following actions:

- FaceTime should be enabled on both your iPhone and iPad.

- Sign in to both devices using the same Apple ID.

- Allow your iPhone to make phone calls to your iPad.

You set up your iPhone first, and then your iPad.

1. Go to Settings > Cellular on your iPhone.

2. Select a line if your iPhone has dual SIM (below Cellular Plans).

3. Take one of the following actions:

- Go to Calls on Additional Devices, turn on Allow Calls on Other Devices, and then choose your iPad and any other devices you want to make and receive calls on.

- When you're near your iPhone and connected to Wi-Fi, this lets your iPad and other devices that are signed in with the same Apple ID to make and receive calls.

- Turn on Add Wi-Fi Calling for Other Devices, then tap Wi-Fi Calling.

This allows you to make and receive calls on your iPad and other Apple ID-enabled devices even if your iPhone isn't nearby.

4. Go to Settings > FaceTime on your iPad, then enable FaceTime and Calls from iPhone. Turn on Wi-Fi Calling if prompted.

You can make and receive phone calls on your iPad after you set up Wi-Fi calling on your iPhone and iPad.

1. Make a phone call: In Contacts, Calendar, FaceTime, Messages, Search, or Safari, tap a phone number. Alternatively, open FaceTime, type in a contact or phone number, and then press.

You get a call: To answer or ignore the call, swipe or tap the notice.

Note: that whether or not you enable Location Services, emergency calls may be made over Wi-Fi, and your device's location information may be utilized for emergency calls to enhance response efforts if you enable Wi-Fi Calling. Some carriers may utilize your location as the address you provided when you signed up for Wi-Fi Calling. Make use of your iPad as a second monitor for your Mac.

You may use Sidecar to increase your Mac's workspace by using an iPad as a second monitor. You can accomplish the following using the expanded workspace:

- Use a variety of apps on various screens.

- On both displays, use the same app. For example, you can utilize Apple Pencil and an app's tools and palettes on iPad while viewing your artwork on your Mac screen.

- Mirror the screens so that the content on the Mac and iPad is the same.

On supported models, Sidecar requires macOS 10.15 or later and iPadOS 13 or later.

Create a Sidecar

1. Make sure your Mac and iPad are both signed in with the same Apple ID.

2. Connect to one of the following:

- Wireless: Make sure Wi-Fi and Bluetooth are turned on your Mac and iPad. They must be in Bluetooth range of each other (about 33 feet or 10 meters).

- USB: Use the proper USB cable to connect your Mac and iPad.

3. On your Mac, go to Apple menu ⬛> System Preferences, choose Displays, and then select your iPad from the bottom left pop-up menu.

Use Sidecar

1. If your iPad isn't already connected, go to Apple menu ⬛> System Preferences, click Displays, and then select your iPad from the pop-up menu at the bottom left.

2. Carry out one of the following actions:

- Switch between screens by dragging a window: Choose "Move to" by dragging the window or holding the cursor over the green button in the top-left corner of the window.

- On the iPad, use the sidebar: ⬛ To show or conceal the menu bar, Dock, ⬛ or keyboard, tap icons in the sidebar with your finger or Apple Pencil. To use keyboard ⬛ shortcuts, press one or more modifier keys, such as Ctrl ⬛.

• To use the Touch Bar on an iPad, tap any button in the Touch Bar with your finger or Apple Pencil. Depending on the software or task, several buttons are available.

• Toggle between the Mac desktop and the iPad Home Screen on the iPad: Swipe up from the bottom edge of your iPad to access the Home Screen. Tap the Sidecar icon in the Dock on your iPad to return to the Mac desktop.

• Rearrange the screens or mirror the displays: Make your settings by going to the Apple menu > System Preferences > Displays.

3. On your iPad, hit the Disconnect symbol at the bottom of the sidebar when you're ready to stop using it. You can also detach from your Mac's Displays preferences.

Cut, copy, and paste on IPad Air 5

You may cut or copy information (a block of text or an image, for example) on your iPad, then paste it on an iPhone, another iPad, iPod touch, or a Mac using Universal Clipboard, and vice versa.

216

Note: See Move and copy items with drag and drop on iPad for information about moving items within an app or copying items across apps on your iPad. See Select, cut, copy, and paste text on iPad for information on cutting, copying, and pasting text exclusively within or across apps on your iPad.

Before you start, make sure you have everything you need. Make sure to follow these steps when cutting or copying and pasting between your iPad and another device:

- On both devices, you're signed in with the same Apple ID.

- Wi-Fi is enabled on your devices.

- Your Bluetooth-enabled gadgets are within range of one another (about 33 feet or 10 meters).

- Handoff is enabled in Settings > General > AirPlay & Handoff on your iPad and another iPadOS or iOS device, and Bluetooth is enabled in Settings.

- Turn on Handoff in System Preferences > General and Bluetooth in System Preferences > Bluetooth on a Mac.

- The following software versions are installed on each device: iOS 10, iPadOS 13, and macOS 10.12 or later are required.

Cut, copy, or paste

- **Copy:** Pinch three fingers together to form a closed fist.

- **Cut:** Twice pinch closed with three fingers.

- **Paste:** Using three fingers, pinch open the paste.

You can also tap Cut, Copy, or Paste after touching and holding a selection.

Important: You only have a limited amount of time to cut, copy, and paste your content.

CHAPTER ELEVEN

ACCESSIBILITY

Get started with the iPad's accessibility features.

The iPad has a variety of accessibility features to help you with your eyesight, physical and motor skills, hearing, and learning. Learn how to set up shortcuts for quick access to these functions.

During setup, enable accessibility features.

When you first set up iPad, you may switch on a lot of accessibility features straight away. After you've turned on your iPad, you can do one of the following things:

- To activate Voiceover, triple-click the Home button (on an iPad with a Home button) or the top button (on an iPad without a Home button) (on other iPad models).

- To activate Zoom, double-tap the screen three times with three fingers.

- Enable Switch Control, Larger Text, and Smart Invert, among other features: Tap 👤 to select a language and country, then select the features you desire. You can also transfer your accessibility

219

settings if you're upgrading from an older iPad. See iPad should be turned on and set up.

Modify the accessibility options

You can alter accessibility settings once you've set up iPad.

1. Select Accessibility from the drop-down menu under Settings.

2. Select one or more of the following features:

- Vision

- VoiceOver

- Zoom

- Display and text size

- Motion

- Spoken content

- Audio descriptions

- Physical and motor

- AssistiveTouch

- Touch accommodations

- Call audio routing

- Face ID and attention

- Switch Control

- Voice Control

- Home or top button

- Apple TV remote

- Pointer control

- Keyboards

- Apple Pencil

- AirPods

- Switch Control

- Voice Control

- Home or top button

- Hearing aids and gadgets

- General

- Guided Access

- Siri

- Accessibility Shortcut

- Per-app settings

- Live Listen

- Sound recognition

- RTT

- Mono audio and balance

- LED flash for notifications

- Headphone accommodations

- Background noises

- Subtitles and captions

- Transcriptions for HomePod Intercom messages

How to turn On Voiceover on IPad Air 5

Even if you can't see the screen, you can use iPad with voice Over, a gesture-based screen reader. From the battery level to who's calling to whatever app your finger is on, VoiceOver provides auditory descriptions of what's on your screen. You can also change the pitch and speaking tempo to suit your preferences. When you touch or drag your finger across the screen, VoiceOver announces the name of the thing you're touching, including icons and text. Use VoiceOver motions to interact with an item, such as a button or link, or to navigate to another item. When you switch to a new screen, VoiceOver makes a sound and then selects and speaks the first item on the screen's name (typically in the top-left corner). When you wake iPad, VoiceOver notifies you when the display changes to landscape or portrait orientation, when the screen dims or locks, and what's active on the Lock Screen.

VoiceOver can be turned on or off.

Important: When you use VoiceOver to manage your iPad, the gestures you use to operate it change. When VoiceOver is turned on, you must operate the iPad using VoiceOver gestures.

Use one of the following techniques to switch VoiceOver on or off:

- Say "Turn on VoiceOver" or "Turn off VoiceOver" to Siri.

- Press the Home button three times (on an iPad with a Home button).

- Press the top button three times (on other iPad models).

- Make use of Control Center.

- Go to Settings ⚙️ > Accessibility > VoiceOver and turn on or off VoiceOver.

VoiceOver gestures should be learned and practiced.

VoiceOver motions can be practiced in a separate area without impacting the iPad or its settings. When you practice a gesture, VoiceOver describes it and the action that follows. Experiment with different strategies to see which one works best for you. If a gesture isn't working, try a faster movement, especially if the motion is a double-tap or swipe. Swipe the screen fast with your finger or fingers to swipe. Touch the screen with some space between your fingers for the greatest results when performing multifinger motions.

1. Go to VoiceOver ⚙️ > Settings > Accessibility.

2. Start by turning on VoiceOver, tapping VoiceOver Practice, and then double-tapping to begin.

3. With one, two, three, and four fingers, practice the following gestures:

- Tap

- Double-tap

- Triple-tap

- Swipe up, down, left, or right

4. Tap Done when you're done practicing, then double-tap to exit.

With the iPad, use hearing aids.

With an iPad, you may alter the settings of Made for iPhone (MFi) hearing aids or sound processors.

Connect an iPad to a hearing aid.

You must pair your hearing equipment with iPad if they are not shown in Settings > Accessibility > Hearing Devices.

1. Remove the battery covers from your hearing aids.

2. Go to Settings > Bluetooth on your iPad, and make sure Bluetooth is switched on.

3. Select Settings > Accessibility > Hearing Devices from the drop-down menu.

4. Turn off your hearing aids and close the battery doors.

5. Tap their names and react to the pairing requests when they appear below MFi Hearing Devices (this may take a minute).

Pairing can take up to 60 seconds, so don't try to stream audio or use the hearing equipment until it's complete. You'll hear a sequence of beeps and a tone when pairing is complete, and a checkmark will display next to the hearing devices in the Devices list. You only have to pair your devices once (and your audiologist might do it for you). After that, whenever you turn on your hearing equipment, they will immediately reconnect to iPad.

You can change the settings and check the status of your hearing aids.

- Go to Settings > Accessibility > Hearing Devices > MFi Hearing Devices in Settings.

- Using keyboard shortcuts for accessibility: On the iPad, see How to Use Accessibility Shortcuts.

- On the Lock Screen, go to Settings > Accessibility > Hearing Devices > MFi Hearing Devices > Control on Lock Screen, then turn it on.

You can accomplish the following from the Lock Screen:

- Examine the battery's condition.

- Adjust the volume and equalization of the surrounding microphone.

- Select whether streaming audio is received by the left, right, or both hearing devices.

- Have complete control over Live Listen.

On the iPad, show transcriptions for HomePod intercom communications. iPad may transcribe Intercom messages for you if members of your household utilize HomePod for Intercom.

1. Open the Home app and go to Home Settings.

2. Select when you want to receive notifications from Intercom by tapping 🏠 it.

3. Select Show Audio Transcriptions under Settings ⚙ > Accessibility > Subtitles & Captioning.

CHAPTER TWELVE

SECURITY AND PRIVACY

Make use of the iPad's built-in security and privacy features.

iPad is built to keep your data and privacy safe. Built-in security mechanisms help protect the data on your iPad and in iCloud from being accessed by anybody other than you. Built-in privacy features limit the amount of information that is accessible to anyone other than you, and you can control what information is shared and where it is shared.

Follow these guidelines to get the most out of the iPad's security and privacy features:

How to make a strong password on your IPad Air 5

The most critical thing you can do to protect your iPad is to set a passcode to open it. See On the iPad, create a passcode.

Use Face ID or Touch ID to unlock your phone.

Face ID (supported models) or Touch ID (supported models) allows you to unlock your iPad, authorize purchases and payments, and sign in to numerous third party apps in a safe and easy manner. See Set up Face ID on your iPad or iPhone. Install Touch ID on your iPad.

Activate Find My iPad.

If your iPad is lost or stolen, Find My can help you locate it and prevent anybody else from activating or using it. See Add your iPad to the Find My section of the app.

Maintain the safety of your Apple ID.

Your Apple ID grants you access to your iCloud data as well as account information for Apple services such as the App Store and Apple Music. See How to Keep Your Apple ID Safe for more information. On iPad, keep your Apple ID safe.

Use When it's ready, sign in with Apple.

Many apps and websites provide Sign in with Apple as a way to make it easier to set up accounts. Signing in with Apple minimizes the amount of information revealed about you, makes it easy to utilize your existing Apple ID, and adds the protection of two-factor authentication. See On the iPad, sign in using your Apple ID.

If Sign in with Apple isn't an option, let iPad create a strong password.

Allow iPad to construct a strong password for you when you sign up for a service on a website or in an app, so you don't have to remember it. See Fill in strong passwords automatically on your iPad. For two-factor authentication, use the built-in authenticator.

On iPad, you can get automatically produced verification tokens for sites and apps that support two-factor authentication instead of relying on SMS messages or third-party apps. See Fill in verification codes on the iPad automatically. You have complete control over the app data and location information you share.

You can change how Apple offers advertising to you in the App Store, Apple News, and Stocks by reviewing and adjusting the data you share with applications, the location information you share, and how Apple sends advertising to you in the App Store, Apple News, and Stocks.

Examine the app's privacy policies.

Before you download an app, look over its privacy policies. For a developer-reported description of the app's privacy practices, including what data is collected, go to the app's product page in the App Store. See On the iPad, you can get apps from the App Store. Examine the App Privacy Report for the apps you download, which displays you how apps are using the rights you provided them and their network activity (iPadOS 15.2 or later). See Examine how apps are making use of the rights you've given them.

Keep your email activity safe.

To make it more difficult for senders to track your Mail activities, enable Mail Privacy Protection. See On the iPad, use Mail Privacy Protection.

Your personal email address should be hidden.

Hide My Email allows you to produce unique, random email addresses that forward to your personal email account when you subscribe to iCloud+. When filling out forms or signing up for newsletters on the web (see Use Hide My Email in Safari on iPad), or when sending email (iPadOS 15.2 or later; see Use Hide My Email in Safari on iPad), you don't have to give your personal email address. On the iPad, use Hide My Email in Mail).

Learn how to protect yourself from harmful websites by better understanding the privacy of your browsing activity in Safari.

Safari makes it difficult for trackers to follow you throughout the internet. You can look at the Privacy

Report to see a list of trackers that Intelligent Tracking Prevention has detected and blocked on the current webpage you're viewing. You can also check and alter Safari settings to keep your browsing activities secret from other users of the same device and to help protect yourself from harmful websites. See Safari on the iPad allows you to browse in private.

App tracking is under your control.

Before monitoring you across applications and websites controlled by other companies to target advertising to you or share your information with a data broker, all apps must acquire your permission. You can alter permissions or stop all apps from asking permission once you grant or refuse permission to an app.

iCloud Private Relay allows you to browse the internet more privately.

You can use iCloud Private Relay (beta) when you subscribe to iCloud+ to help prevent websites and network providers from developing a detailed profile about you. When you enable iCloud Private Relay, all traffic leaving your iPad is encrypted and routed through two different internet relays. Websites won't be able to view your IP address or location, and network providers won't be able to gather your browsing history. A website or a network provider will not know both who you are and which websites you visit at the same time. See On your iPad, enable iCloud Private Relay.

Create a passcode on your iPad.

Set a passcode that must be input to unlock iPad when it is turned on or woken up for more security. Data protection is enabled by setting a passcode, which secures your iPad data with 256-bit AES encryption. Set or modify the passcode (certain apps may not use data protection.)

1. Go to Settings, then tap one of the following options, depending on your model:

- Passcode and Face ID

- Passcode and Touch ID

2. Select Turn Passcode On or Change Passcode from the drop-down menu.

Tap Passcode Choices to see the password-creation options. Custom Alphanumeric Code and Custom Numeric Code are the most secure options. After you've set a passcode, you can unlock your iPad with Face ID or Touch ID on supported models. However, under the following circumstances, you must always enter your passcode to unlock your iPad for added security:

- You switch your iPad **on or restart it.**

- It's been more than 48 hours since you've unlocked your iPad.

- You haven't used the passcode to unlock your iPad in the last 6.5 days, and you haven't used Face ID or Touch ID in the last 4 hours.

- A remote lock command is sent to your iPad.

- You've tried five times with Face ID or Touch ID to unlock your iPad without success.

Change the time when the iPad locks automatically.

Set a timer for Auto-Lock under Settings > Display & Brightness > Auto-Lock.

After ten failed passcodes, the data is erased.

After 10 failed passcode tries, configure iPad to wipe all information, media, and personal settings.

1. Go to Settings, then tap one of the following options, depending on your model:

- Touch ID & Passcode

- Passcode

- Face ID & Passcode

2. Select Erase Data from the menu.

You must restore iPad from a backup or set it up as new after all data has been deleted.

Disable the passcode

1. Go to Settings, then tap one of the following options, depending on your model:

- Touch ID & Passcode

- Passcode

- Face ID & Passcode

2. Select Turn Passcode Off from the drop-down menu.

Passcode must be reset.

You'll be locked out of your device and receive a notice saying iPad is disabled if you enter the wrong passcode six times in a row. If you forget your passcode, you can use a computer or recovery mode to delete your iPad and set a new one. (If you backed up your data and settings to iCloud or your computer before forgetting your passcode, you can restore them from the backup.)

Install Face ID on your iPad.

Face ID (supported models) lets you securely unlock your iPad, authorize purchases and payments, and sign in to a variety of third-party apps by merely gazing at it.

You must also set a passcode on your iPad to use Face ID.

Set up Face ID or change your appearance.

- Go to Settings ⚙ > Face ID & Passcode > Set up Face ID, then follow the onscreen instructions if you didn't set up Face ID when you first set up your iPad.

- •Go to Settings ⚙ > Face ID & Passcode > Set Up an Other Appearance, then follow the onscreen steps to set up an alternate appearance for Face ID to identify.

During Face ID setup, you can tap Accessibility Options if you have physical constraints. Setting up facial recognition in this manner does not necessitate the use of the entire range of head movements. Face ID is still safe, but it necessitates a more consistent way of looking at the iPad. If you're blind or have low eyesight, Face ID offers an accessibility function that you can use. Go to Settings ⚙ > Accessibility > Face ID & Attention, then turn off Require Attention for Face ID if you don't want Face ID to require you to look at your iPad with your eyes open. If you enable VoiceOver when you first set up your iPad, this feature is disabled. See On the iPad, adjust the Face ID and attentiveness settings.

Disable Face ID for the time being.

You can disable Face ID on your iPad for a limited time.

1. For 2 seconds, press and hold the top and volume buttons simultaneously.

2. When the sliders show, tap the top button to lock the iPad right away.

If you don't touch the screen for a minute or more, the iPad will automatically lock. Face ID is activated again the next time you unlock your iPad with your passcode.

Face ID should be turned off.

1. Go to Face ID & Passcode ⚙ > Settings > Face ID & Passcode.

2. Select one of the following options:

- Disable Face ID exclusively for certain items: One or more of the options can be turned off.

- Disable Face ID: Reset Face ID by pressing the Reset Face ID button.

With Find My iPhone Lost Mode, you can block Face ID from being used to unlock your device if it is lost or stolen. (For more information, see Add your iPad to Find My.)

Install Touch ID on your iPad.

Use Touch ID to securely and conveniently unlock iPad, approve purchases and payments, and sign in to numerous third-party apps on an iPad with a Home button, iPad Air (4th generation and later), or iPad mini (6th generation).

Make fingerprint recognition active.

1. Go to Settings > Touch ID & Passcode if you didn't turn on fingerprint recognition when you originally set up your iPad.

2. Select one of the alternatives and follow the on-screen directions.

When you first purchase something from the App Store, Apple Books, or the iTunes Store after turning on iTunes & App Store, you'll be asked for your Apple ID password. You'll be asked to utilize Touch ID on your next purchase.

Note: If you're having trouble adding a fingerprint or utilizing Touch ID to unlock your iPad, visit this Apple Support post. If Touch ID isn't working, go to the next step.

Put a fingerprint on it.

You can add as many fingerprints as you want (both of your thumbs and forefingers, for example).

1. Go to Touch ID & Passcode > Settings.

2. Select Add a Fingerprint from the drop-down menu.

3. Follow the directions on the screen.

A fingerprint can be given a name or it can be removed.

1. Go to Touch ID & Passcode > Settings.

If you have more than one fingerprint, you can identify each one by doing one of the following:

- If your iPad has a Home button, place your finger on it.

- Rest a finger on the top button on an iPad mini (6th generation) or iPad Air (4th generation and later).

2. Tap the fingerprint, then either give it a name (such as "Thumb") or delete it.

Disable Touch ID.

Turn off one or more of the options under Settings > Touch ID & Passcode.

Control who has access to information in iPad apps.

You have complete control over whether third-party apps have access to your Contacts, Photos, Calendar, and other apps. App access to information should be reviewed or changed. You'll get a request with an explanation the first time an app requests to borrow data from another app. A messaging app, for example, can ask for access to your contacts in order to discover pals who use the same service. You can adjust access later after you grant or refuse it.

1. Go to Privacy > Settings.

2. Select a type of information, such as Calendars, Reminders, or Motion & Fitness from the drop-down menu. The following is a list of the apps that have requested access. Any app on the list can have access turned on or off.

Examine how apps are making use of the rights you've given them.

Navigate to Settings > Privacy > App Privacy Report (iPadOS 15.2 or later). The App Privacy Report shows you how apps are using the rights you gave them and how they are using the internet.

Go to Settings > Privacy > App Privacy Report, then hit Turn Off App Privacy Report to disable the report and delete its data. You can turn the report back on by returning to this Settings screen.

CHAPTER 13

SAFETY, HANDLING AND SUPPORT

WARNING: Failure to follow these safety precautions may result in a fire, electric shock, injury, or damage to your iPad or other property. Before you use iPad, make sure you read all of the safety advice included below.

Handling: Handle the iPad with caution. It's comprised of metal, glass, and plastic, and it's filled with very sensitive electronic components. If the iPad is dropped, burned, punctured, or crushed, or if it comes into touch with fluids, it can be damaged. If you believe that your iPad or battery has been damaged, you should stop using it immediately to avoid overheating or harm. If your iPad's screen is cracked, don't use it because it could cause you harm. Consider using a case or cover if you're worried about scratching the iPad's surface.

Repairing: Don't open the iPad and don't try to fix it yourself. If you disassemble your iPad, you risk damaging it or injuring yourself. Touch Apple or an Apple Authorized Service Provider if your iPad is damaged, malfunctions, or comes into contact with liquid. Repairs performed by companies other than Apple or an Apple

Authorized Service Provider may not employ Apple genuine parts, compromising the device's safety and performance. The iPad Repair page has further information regarding repairs and service.

Battery: Don't try to change the iPad battery on your own. Apple or an authorized service provider should service or recycle the lithium-ion battery in the iPad. Improper service can harm the battery, cause it to overheat, and even cause injury. The battery must be recycled or disposed of separately from regular garbage. Don't let the batteries catch fire. Visit the Battery Service and Recycling website for more information on battery services and recycling.

Lasers: One or more lasers are used in the TrueDepth camera system and the LiDAR Scanner. If the equipment is damaged or malfunctions, these laser systems may be disabled for safety reasons. You should always have your iPad serviced by Apple or an authorized service provider if you receive a notification that the laser system is disabled on your iPad. Improper repair, modification, or use of non-genuine Apple components in laser systems may cause the safety measures to malfunction, resulting in dangerous exposure and skin harm.

Distraction: In some cases, utilizing an iPad may cause you to become distracted and put you in a risky scenario (for example, avoid using headphones while riding a bicycle and avoid typing a text message while driving a car). Follow any guidelines that prohibit or limit the use of cell phones or headphones.

Data services are required for Navigation Maps to function. Because these data services are subject to change and may not be available in all countries or regions, maps and location-based information may be unavailable, inaccurate, or incomplete. Compare the information in Maps to your current location.

Navigation: use common sense. To settle any inconsistencies, always keep an eye on the current road conditions and posted signs. Some Maps features necessitate the use of Location Services.

Charging: with the accompanying USB cord and power converter, you can charge your iPad. You can also charge iPad with "Made for iPad" or other third-party USB 2.0 or later cables and power adapters that comply with applicable local requirements as well as international and regional safety standards. Other adapters may not fulfill applicable safety standards, putting you at danger of death or harm if you charge with them. Using faulty cords or chargers, or charging while wet, can result in fire, electric shock, injury, or damage to your iPad or other property. Before plugging the power adapter into a wall socket to charge your iPad, ensure sure the USB cable is fully attached. When not in use or charging, keep the iPad, USB cable, and power adapter in a well-ventilated location.

Connector: and charging cord When the charging cable is connected to a power source, avoid prolonged skin contact with the charging cable and connector to avoid irritation or harm. It is not a good idea to sleep or sit on the charging cord or connector.

Long-term heat exposure: The surface temperature restrictions set by applicable country requirements as well as international and regional safety standards are met by the iPad and its USB power adapter. Even within these boundaries, prolonged contact with warm surfaces for lengthy periods of time can cause discomfort or harm. When a device or its power adapter is working or connected to a power source for long periods of time, use common sense to prevent coming into touch with your skin. When a gadget or power adapter is attached to a power source, don't sleep on it or put it beneath a blanket, pillow, or your body. When not in use or charging, keep your iPad and its power adapter in a well-ventilated place. If you have a physical condition that limits your capacity to perceive heat against the body, take extra precautions.

USB power: supply Plug the Apple USB power adapter directly into a power outlet to run it safely and limit the risk of heat-related injury or damage. Avoid using the power adapter near a sink, bathtub, or shower stall, and avoid connecting or disconnecting the power adapter with wet hands. If any of the following situations present, stop using the power adapter and any cables:

- The plug or prongs on the power adapter are broken.

- The charge cable becomes frayed or damaged in any other way.

- The power adapter has been exposed to excessive dampness or has had liquid spilled into it.

- The power adapter's housing has been shattered after it was dropped.

Specifications for the USB power adaptor are as follows:

• Frequency	50-60 Hz, single phase	
• Line voltage	100 to 240 vac	
• Output voltage	Refer to the output marking in the power adapter	

Hearing loss: is a common problem. Hearing loss might occur if you listen to music at a high volume. Background noise and long-term exposure to high volume levels can make sounds appear quieter than they are. Before you put anything in your ear, turn on the audio and check the volume. Reduce loud headphone sounds in Settings for information on how to set a maximum volume limit on iPad. Visit the Sound and Hearing page for additional information on hearing loss. The dark insulating rings on the plugs of the Apple headsets marketed with iPhone in China are meant to conform with Chinese requirements and are only compatible with iPad, iPhone, and iPod touch.

WARNING: Do not listen to music at excessive volume levels for lengthy periods of time to avoid hearing harm.

Exposure: to radio frequencies to connect to wireless networks, the iPad employs radio signals. Go to Settings ⚙️ > General > Legal & Regulatory > RF Exposure or visit the RF Exposure page for more information about radio frequency (RF) energy emitted by radio waves and steps you may take to reduce your exposure.

Interference with radio frequencies Keep an eye out for signs and notifications prohibiting or restricting the use of mobile devices. Despite the fact that the iPad was developed, tested, and built to conform with radio frequency emission rules, the iPad's emissions can interfere with the operation of other electronic equipment, leading it to malfunction. Turn off iPad or use airplane mode or Settings ⚙️ > Wi-Fi and Settings > Bluetooth to turn off the iPad wireless transmitters when use is forbidden, such as while flying by plane or when instructed to do so by authorities.

Interference with medical devices: Magnets, as well as components and/or radios that create electromagnetic fields, are found in the iPad, iPad Smart Cover, Smart Folio, Smart Keyboard Folio, Magic Keyboard for iPad, and Apple Pencil. Medical instruments may be harmed by these magnets and electromagnetic radiation. Consult your physician and the maker of your medical device for information about your device, including if you need to keep a safe distance between it and your iPad, iPad Smart Cover, Smart Folio, Smart Keyboard Folio, Magic Keyboard for iPad, or Apple Pencil. To avoid any interference, manufacturers frequently provide guidelines on how to safely operate their gadgets around wireless or magnetic products. Stop using the iPad, iPad Smart Cover, Smart Folio, Smart Keyboard Folio, Magic Keyboard for iPad, or Apple Pencil if you feel they're interfering with your medical device.

Sensors in medical devices such as implanted pacemakers and defibrillators may respond to magnets and radios when they are in close proximity. Keep your iPad, iPad Smart Cover, Smart Folio, Smart Keyboard Folio, Magic Keyboard for iPad, and Apple Pencil a safe distance away from your device (more than 6 inches/15cm, but consult your physician and device manufacturer for specific guidelines) to avoid any potential interactions with these devices. This is not a medical device. The iPad is not a medical gadget, and it should not be used to replace expert medical advice. It is not intended for use in the diagnosis of disease or other disorders, nor in the treatment, mitigation, or prevention of any condition or disease. Please consult your healthcare practitioner before making any health-related decisions. Medical problems Consult your physician before using iPad if you have a medical condition or are experiencing symptoms that you feel could be caused by iPad or flashing lights (for example, seizures, blackouts, eyestrain, or migraines). Explosive and other types of weather Charging or using an iPad in a potentially explosive environment, such as one with high amounts of flammable chemicals, gases, or particles (such as grain, dust, or metal powders), can be dangerous. iPad operation may be damaged or impaired if it is exposed to situations with high concentrations of industrial chemicals, such as near evaporating liquefied gasses like helium.

All signs and instructions must be followed.

Motion that is repeated You may suffer discomfort in your hands, arms, wrists, shoulders, neck, or other portions of your body when you conduct repeated tasks on your iPad, including as typing, swiping, or playing games. Stop using the iPad and see a doctor if you're experiencing any pain. Activities with a lot of ramifications This device is not intended for use in situations where its failure could result in death, personal harm, or significant environmental damage. Risk of choking Some iPad accessories could cause choking in little children. Keep these items out of reach of tiny children.

iPad is programmed to lock after two minutes of inactivity to save energy. Go to Settings > Display & Brightness > Auto-Lock, then choose an option. Press the top button or the Home button to unlock an iPad with a Home button. Other iPad models can be unlocked by tapping the screen or pressing the top button.

The ENERGY STAR criteria for energy efficiency are met by the iPad. Reduced energy consumption saves money and aids in the conservation of vital resources; see the Energy Star website for more information.

Important iPad handling information

Cleaning If your iPad comes into touch with anything that could cause stains or other harm, such as dirt or sand, ink, makeup, soap, detergent, acids or acidic foods, or lotions, clean it right away.

- Disconnect all wires, then switch off iPad using one of the following methods:

- Press and hold the top button on an iPad with a Home button until the slider displays, then drag the slider.

- On other iPad models, press and hold the top and volume buttons simultaneously until the sliders display, then drag the top slider.

- Every model: Drag the slider under Settings > General > Shut Down.

- Avoid getting moisture in openings by using a soft, slightly damp, lint-free cloth—for example, a lens cloth.

- Avoid using cleaning supplies or pressurized air.

The front of the iPad is constructed of glass with an oleophobic (oil-repellent) fingerprint-resistant coating. With typical use, this covering wears away. Cleaning chemicals and abrasive materials will eat away at the coating and perhaps scratch the glass. Connectors, ports, and buttons are used. Never force a connector into a port or press down too hard on a button, since this could result in damage that isn't covered by the warranty. If the connection and port don't fit together easily, they're probably not compatible. Check for obstructions and double-check that the connector is compatible with the port and that it is positioned correctly in relation to the port.

USB to Lightning Cable (models with a Lightning connector) It's common for the Lightning connector to discolor after a long period of use. Discoloration can be caused by dirt, debris, and moisture exposure. Disconnect your iPad from your computer or power adapter and wipe the Lightning connector with a soft, dry, lint-free cloth if your Lightning cable or connector becomes warm during usage or if your iPad won't charge or sync. When cleaning the Lightning connector, avoid using liquids or cleaning agents. USB-C Charge Cable or Lightning to USB Cable (depending on model) Fraying or breaking of cables can be caused by certain usage patterns. If repeatedly bent in the same area, the supplied cable, like any other metal wire or cable, will become weak or brittle. Instead of angles, aim for soft curves in the cable. Inspect the cable and connector for kinks, breaks, bends, or other damage on a regular basis. If you notice any such damage, you should stop using the cable.

Temperature in use iPad is designed to work in temperatures ranging from 32° to 95° F (0° to 35° C) and be stored in temperatures ranging from -4° to 113° F (-20° to 45° C). If you store or use your iPad outside of these temperature ranges, it can be damaged and your battery life will be limited. Avoid exposing the iPad to extreme temperature or humidity changes. It's typical for iPad to grow warm whether you're using it or charging the battery. If the inside temperature of your iPad rises over normal operating temperatures (for example, if you leave it in a hot car or in direct sunlight for a lengthy period of time), you may notice the following symptoms as it tries to cool down:

- The iPad's charging stops.

- The monitor dims.

- A temperature warning shows on the screen.

- Some apps may be forced to close.

Important: While the temperature warning screen is visible, you may not be able to use your iPad. If the iPad's internal temperature is too high, it goes into deep sleep mode until it cools down. Wait a few minutes after moving iPad to a cooler position out of direct sunlight before attempting to use it again.

Statement of FCC compliance

Part 15 of the FCC Rules applies to this device. This device's functioning is subject to two conditions: (1) it may not cause harmful interference, and (2) it must accept any interference it receives, including interference that may cause undesired operation.

Note: According to part 15 of the FCC Rules, this equipment has been tested and determined to conform with the restrictions for a Class B digital device. In a home installation, these restrictions are intended to provide reasonable protection against hazardous interference. This equipment generates, utilizes, and can radiate radio frequency energy and may cause detrimental interference to radio communications if not installed and used according to the instructions. However, no guarantee can be made that interference will not occur in a specific installation.

If this device does cause harmful interference to radio or television reception, which can be determined by turning it on and off, the user is urged to try one or more of the following actions to rectify the interference:

- Adjust the receiving antenna's position or relocate it.

- Increase the distance between the receiver and the equipment.

- Plug the equipment into an outlet on a different circuit than the receiver.

- Seek advice from a dealer or an experienced radio/TV technician.

Unauthorized changes or modifications to this product may nullify the electromagnetic compatibility (EMC) and wireless compliance, as well as your authority to use it.

This product has demonstrated EMC compliance in the presence of compliant peripheral devices and shielded cables connecting system components. To avoid introducing interference to radios, televisions, and other electronic devices, make sure you utilize compatible peripheral devices and shielded cables between system components.

Printed in Great Britain
by Amazon

86292814R00150